☞ **W9-BUK-244**

Simply *Shakespeare*

Original Shakespearean Text
With a Modern Line-for-Line Translation

TWELFTH NIGHT

BARRON'S

All inquiries should be addressed to:
Barron's Educational Series, Inc.
250 Wireless Boulevard
Hauppauge, New York 11788
http://www.barronseduc.com

ISBN 10: 0-7641-2088-3
ISBN 13: 978-0-7641-2088-6

Library of Congress Catalog Card No. 2001043293

Library of Congress Cataloging-in-Publication Data

Shakespeare, William, 1564–1616.
     Twelfth night / edited and rendered into modern English by Fitzgerald Higgins.
          p. cm. — (Simply Shakespeare)
     Includes bibliographical references.
     Summary: Presents the original text of Shakespeare's play side by side with a
     modern version, with discussion questions, role-playing scenarios, and other
     study activities.
     ISBN 0-7641-2088-3
          1. Survival after airplane accidents, shipwrecks, etc.—Juvenile drama.
     2. Brothers and sisters—Juvenile drama. 3. Illyria—Juvenile drama. 4. Twins—
     Juvenile drama. 5. Children's plays, English. [1. Shakespeare, William,
     1564–1616. Twelfth night. 2. Plays. 3. English literature—History and criti-
     cism.] I. Higgins, Fitzgerald. II. Title.

PR2837.A25 2002
822.3'3—dc21

                                                                        2001043293

PRINTED IN CHINA
19 18 17 16 15 14 13 12 11

Simply Shakespeare

Titles in the Series

Contents

Introduction

William Shakespeare, 1564–1616

Who was William Shakespeare? This simple question has challenged scholars for years. The man behind vivid, unforgettable characters like Hamlet, Romeo and Juliet, and King Lear is a shadow compared to his creations. Luckily, official records of Shakespeare's time have preserved some facts about his life.

Shakespeare was born in April 1564 in Stratford-upon-Avon, England. His father, John Shakespeare, was a prominent local merchant. Shakespeare probably attended grammar school in Stratford, learning basic Latin and Greek and studying works by ancient Roman writers. In 1582, when Shakespeare was 18, he married Anne Hathaway. Eventually, the couple had three children—but, like many families in their day, they were forced to endure a tragic loss when Hamnet, their only son, died at age 11.

No records document Shakespeare's life from 1585 to 1592, when he was between the ages of 21 and 28. In his writings, Shakespeare seems to know so much about so many things that it's tempting to make guesses about how he supported his young family during this period. Over the years, it's been speculated that he worked as a schoolteacher, a butcher, or an actor—and even that he did a little poaching as a young man. Thanks to some London theater gossip left behind by a professional rival, we know that Shakespeare was living in London as a playwright and an actor by 1592. Meanwhile, Anne and the children stayed in Stratford.

This must have been a thrilling time for Shakespeare. In 1592, England was becoming a powerful nation under its great and clever queen, Elizabeth I. English explorers and colonists crossed seas to search strange new worlds. London was a bustling, exciting center of commerce, full of travelers from abroad. And though many Europeans still looked down on English culture, they admitted that London's stages boasted some of the best plays and actors to be found. Travelers from all over admired the dramas of Christopher Marlowe, Thomas Kyd, and the new name on the scene, William Shakespeare.

Nevertheless, the life of the theater had its hazards. London's actors, playwrights, and theatrical entrepreneurs chose a risky and somewhat shady line of work. Religious leaders condemned the theater for encouraging immorality and idleness among the London populace. London's city leaders, fearful of crowds, closed the theaters in times of unrest or plague. Luckily, the London troupes had some powerful "fans"—members of the nobility who acted as patrons, protecting the troupes from their enemies. Queen Elizabeth herself loved plays. Special performances were regularly given for her at court.

By 1594, two theatrical companies had emerged as the most popular. Archrivals, The Lord Admiral's Men and The Lord Chamberlain's Men performed at the Rose and the Theatre, respectively. However, The Lord Chamberlain's Men had an ace: Shakespeare was both a founding member and the company's main playwright. The company's fine lead actor was Richard Burbage, the first man to play such roles as Hamlet, Othello, and Macbeth. With a one-two punch like that, it's not surprising that The Lord Chamberlain's Men soon emerged as London's top troupe. By 1597, Shakespeare had written such works as *Romeo and Juliet, The Merchant of Venice,* and *A Midsummer Night's Dream.* His finances grew with his reputation, and he was able to buy land and Stratford's second-largest house, where Anne and the children moved while he remained in London.

Then as now, owning property went a long way. Like many acting companies to this day, The Lord Chamberlain's Men got involved in a bitter dispute with their landlord. However, they owned the actual timbers of the Theatre building—which turned out to be useful assets. Eventually the exasperated troupe hired a builder to secretly take apart the Theatre, then transported its timbers across London to the south bank of the River Thames. There, they used the Theatre's remains to construct their new home—The Globe.

At The Globe, many of Shakespeare's greatest plays first came to life. From 1599 until his death in 1616, the open-air Globe served as Shakespeare's main stage. Audiences saw the first performances of *Hamlet, Macbeth, Twelfth Night,* and *King Lear* there. (In winter, Shakespeare's company performed at London's Blackfriars, the indoor theater that housed the first performance of *The Tempest.*) In 1603, after the death of Queen Elizabeth, Shakespeare's troupe added a new triumph to its résumé. Changing its name to The King's Men, it became the official theatrical company of England's new monarch, James I. The company performed frequently at court and state functions for its powerful new patron.

Around 1611–1612, Shakespeare returned permanently to Stratford. Unfortunately, we know little about his domestic life there. Where Shakespeare is concerned, there's no "tell-all" biography to reveal his intimate life. Was he happily wed to Anne, or did he live for so long in London to escape a bad marriage? Do the sonnets Shakespeare published in 1609 tell us a real-life story of his relationships with a young man, a "Dark Lady," and a rival for the lady's love? What were Shakespeare's political beliefs? From his writings, it's clear that Shakespeare understood life's best and worst emotions very deeply. But we'll never know how much of his own life made its way into his art. He died at the age of 53 on April 23, 1616, leaving behind the almost 40 plays and scores of poems that have spoken for him to generations of readers and listeners. Shakespeare is buried in Holy Trinity Church in Stratford, where he lies under a stone that warns the living—in verse—never to disturb his bones.

Shakespeare's Theater

Going to a play in Shakespeare's time was a completely different experience than going to a play today. How theaters were built, who attended, what happened during the performance, and who produced the plays were all quite unlike most theater performances today.

Theaters in Shakespeare's time were mainly outside the walls of the city of London—and away from the authorities *in* London. In those times, many religious authorities (especially radical Protestants) condemned plays and playgoing. They preached that plays, being stage illusions, were acts of deception and therefore sinful. The city authorities in London agreed that the theaters encouraged immorality. Despite this, theaters did exist in and around the city of London. They were, however, housed in neighborhoods known as Liberties. Liberties were areas that previously had religious functions and therefore were under the control of the crown, not the city of London. Luckily for playgoers, the monarchs Elizabeth and James were more tolerant of the amusements offered by the stage than the London authorities.

Who enjoyed what the stage had to offer? Almost all of London society went to the theater. Merchants and their wives, prostitutes, lawyers, laborers, and visitors from other countries would attend. Once you were at the theater, your social station dictated what you could pay and where you sat. If you could only afford a pence (about a penny), you would stand in the yard immediately surrounding the stage.

(These members of Shakespeare's audience were called "groundlings.") As many as a thousand other spectators might join you there. In the yard everyone would be exposed to the weather and to peddlers selling fruit and nuts. Your experience would probably be more active and less quiet than attending a play today. Movement was not uncommon. If you wanted a better or different view, you might rove about the yard. If you paid another pence, you could move into a lower gallery.

The galleries above and surrounding the stage on all sides could accommodate up to 2,000 more people. However, because the galleries were vertical and surrounded the stage, no matter where you sat, you would never be more than 35 feet away from the stage. The galleries immediately behind the stage were reserved for members of the nobility and royalty. From behind the stage a noble could not only see everything, but—more importantly—could be seen by others in the audience! Queen Elizabeth and King James were less likely to attend a theater performance, although they protected theater companies. Instead, companies performed plays for them at court.

The Globe's stage was similar to the other outdoor theaters in Shakespeare's time. These stages offered little decoration or frills. Consequently, the actors and the text carried the burden of delivering the drama. Without the help of scenery or lighting, the audience had to imagine what was not represented on the stage (the storms, shipwrecks, and so forth). The Globe's stage was rectangular—with dimensions of about 27 by 44 feet. At the back of the stage was a curtained wall containing three entrances onto the stage. These entrances led directly from the tiring (as in "attiring") house, where the actors would dress. The middle entrance was covered by a hanging tapestry and was probably used for special entrances—such as a ceremonial procession or the delivery of a prologue.

Unlike the yard, the stage was covered by a canopied roof that was suspended by two columns. This canopy was known as the *heavens*. Its underside was covered with paintings of the sun, moon, stars, and sky and was visible to all theatergoers. *Hell* was the area below the stage with a trapdoor as the entrance. Immediately behind and one flight above the stage were the dressing rooms, and above them lay the storage area for props and costumes.

Indoor theaters were similar to outdoor theaters in many respects. They featured a bare stage with the heavens, a trapdoor leading to hell, and doors leading to the tiring house. Builders created indoor theaters from preexisting space in already constructed buildings. These theaters were smaller, and because they were in town they were also more expensive. Standing in the yard of an outdoor theater cost a pence. The cheapest seat in an *indoor* theater was sixpence. The most fashionable and wealthy members of London society attended indoor theaters as much to see as to be seen. If you were a gallant (a fashionable theater-goer), you could pay 24 pence and actually sit on a stool at the edge of the stage—where everyone could see you.

The actors' costumes were also on display. Whether plays were performed indoors or outdoors, costumes were richly decorated. They were one of the main assets of a theater company and one of the draws of theater. However, costumes didn't necessarily match the period of the play's setting. How spectacular the costumes looked was more important than how realistic they were or if they matched the period setting.

These costumes were worn on stage only by men or boys who were a part of licensed theater companies. The actors in the companies were exclusively male and frequently doubled up on parts. Boys played female roles before their voices changed. Some actors were also shareholders—the most important members of a theater company. The shareholders owned the company's assets (the play texts, costumes, and props) and made a profit from the admissions gathered. Besides the shareholders and those actors who did not hold shares, other company members were apprentices and hired men and musicians.

The actors in Shakespeare's day worked hard. They were paid according to the house's take. New plays were staged rapidly, possibly with as little as three weeks from the time a company first received the play text until opening night. All the while, the companies appeared to have juggled a large number of new and older plays in performance. In lead roles, the most popular actors might have delivered as many as 4,000 lines in six different plays during a London working week! Working at this pace, it seems likely that teamwork was key to a company's success.

The Sound of Shakespeare

Shakespeare's heroes and heroines all share one quality: They're all great talkers. They combine Shakespeare's powerful imagery and vocabulary with a sound that thunders, trills, rocks, and sings.

When Shakespearean actors say their lines, they don't just speak lines of dialogue. Often, they're also speaking lines of dramatic poetry that are written in a sound pattern called *iambic pentameter*. When these lines don't rhyme and are not grouped in stanzas, they're called *blank verse*. Though many passages in Shakespeare plays are written in prose, the most important and serious moments are almost always in iambic pentameter. As Shakespeare matured, the sound of his lines began to change. Late plays like *The Tempest* are primarily in a wonderfully flowing blank verse. Earlier works, such as *Romeo and Juliet,* feature much more rhymed iambic pentameter, often with punctuation at the end of each line to make the rhymes even stronger.

Terms like "iambic pentameter" sound scarily technical—like part of a chemistry experiment that will blow up the building if you measure it wrong. But the Greeks, who invented iambic pentameter, used it as a dance beat. Later writers no longer used it as something one could literally shimmy to, but it was still a way to organize the rhythmic noise and swing of speech. An *iamb* contains one unaccented (or unstressed) syllable and one accented (stressed) syllable, in that order. It borrows from the natural swing of our heartbeats to go *ker-THUMP, ker-THUMP.* Five of these ker-thumping units in a row make a line of iambic *penta*meter.

Dance or rock music needs a good, regular thumping of drums (or drum machine) and bass to get our feet tapping and bodies dancing, but things can get awfully monotonous if that's all there is to the sound. Poetry works the same way. With its ten syllables and five ker-thumps, a line like "he WENT to TOWN toDAY to BUY a CAR" is perfect iambic pentameter. It's just as regular as a metronome. But it isn't poetry. "In SOOTH/ I KNOW/ not WHY/ I AM/ so SAD" is poetry (*The Merchant of Venice*, Act 1, Scene 1). Writers like Shakespeare change the iambic pentameter pattern of their blank verse all the time to keep things sounding interesting. The melody of vowels and other sound effects makes the lines even more musical and varied. As it reaches the audience's ears, this mix of basic, patterned beat and sound variations carries powerful messages of meaning and emotion. The beating, regular rhythms of blank verse also help actors remember their lines.

Why did Shakespeare use this form? Blank verse dominated through a combination of novelty, tradition, and ease. The Greeks and Romans passed on a tradition of combining poetry and drama. English playwrights experimented with this tradition by using all sorts of verse and prose for their plays. By the 1590s, blank verse had caught on with some of the best new writers in London. In the hands of writers like the popular Christopher Marlowe and the up-and-coming Will Shakespeare, it was more than just the latest craze in on-stage sound.

Blank verse also fit well with the English language itself. Compared to languages like French and Italian, English is hard to rhyme. It's also heavily accentual—another way of saying that English really bumps and thumps.

The words and sounds coming from the stage were new and thrilling to Shakespeare's audience. England was falling in love with its own language. English speakers were still making up grammar, spelling, and pronunciation as they went along—giving the language more of a "hands-on" feel than it has today. The grammar books and dictionaries that finally fixed the "rules" of English did not appear until after Shakespeare's death. The language grew and grew, soaking up words from other languages, combining and making new words. Politically, the country also grew in power and pride.

Shakespeare's language reflects this sense of freedom, experimentation, and power. When he put his words in the beat of blank verse and the mouths of London's best actors, it must have sounded a little like the birth of rock and roll—mixing old styles and new sounds to make a new, triumphant swagger.

Publishing Shakespeare

Books of Shakespeare's plays come in all shapes and sizes. They range from slim paperbacks like this one to heavy, muscle-building anthologies of his collected works. Libraries devote shelves of space to works by and about "the Bard." Despite all that paper and ink, no printed text of a Shakespeare play can claim to be an exact, word-by-word copy of what Shakespeare wrote.

Today, most writers work on computers and can save their work electronically. Students everywhere know the horror of losing the only copy of something they've written and make sure they always have a backup version! In Shakespeare's time, a playwright delivered a handwritten copy of his work to the acting company that asked him to write a play. This may have been his only copy—which was now the property of the company, not the writer. In general, plays were viewed as mere "entertainments"—not literary art. They were written quickly and were often disposed of when the acting companies had no more use for them.

The draft Shakespeare delivered was a work in progress. He and the company probably added, deleted, and changed some material—stage directions, entrances and exits, even lines and character names—during rehearsals. Companies may have had a clean copy written out by a scribe (a professional hand-writer) or by the writer himself. Most likely they kept this house copy for future performances. No copies of Shakespeare's plays in his own handwriting have survived.

Acting companies might perform a hit play for years before it was printed, usually in small books called *quartos*. However, the first published versions of Shakespeare's plays vary considerably. Some of these texts are thought to be of an inferior, incomplete quality. Because of this, scholars have speculated that they are not based on authoritative, written copies, but were re-created from actors' memories or from the shorthand notes of a scribe working for a publisher.

Shakespearean scholars often call these apparently faulty versions of his plays "bad quartos." Why might such texts have appeared? Scholars have guessed that they are "pirated versions." They believe that acting companies tried to keep their plays out of print to prevent rival troupes from stealing popular material. However, booksellers sometimes printed unauthorized versions of Shakespeare's plays that were used by competing companies. The pirated versions may have been done with help from actors who had played minor roles in the play, memorized it, and then sold their unreliable, memorized versions. (In recent years, this theory has been challenged by some scholars who argue that the "bad" quartos may be based on Shakespeare's own first drafts or that they reliably reflect early performance texts of the plays.)

"Good" quartos were printed with the permission of the company that owned the play and were based on written copies. However, even these authorized versions were far from perfect. The printers had to work either by deciphering the playwright's handwriting or by using a flawed version printed earlier. They also had to memorize lines as they manually set type on the press. And they decided how a line should be punctuated and spelled—not always with foolproof judgment!

The first full collection of Shakespeare's plays came out in 1623, seven years after his death. Called the "First Folio," this collection included 36 plays compiled by John Heminge and Henry Condell, actor-friends of Shakespeare from The King's Men troupe.

To develop the First Folio texts, Heminge, Condell, and their co-editors probably worked with a mix of handwritten and both good and bad printed versions of their friend's plays. Their 1623 version had many errors, and though later editions of that text corrected some mistakes, they also added new ones. The First Folio also contained no indications of where acts and scenes began and ended. The scene and act divisions that appear standard in most modern editions of Shakespeare actually rely on the shrewd guesses of generations of editors and researchers.

Most modern editors of Shakespeare depend on a combination of trustworthy early publications to come up with the most accurate text possible. They often use the versions in the First Folio, its later editions, and other "good," authorized publications of single plays. In some cases, they also consult "bad" versions or rely on pure guesswork to decide the most likely reading of some words or lines. Because of such uncertainties, modern editions of Shakespeare often vary, depending on editors' research and choices.

Twelfth Night

Introduction to the Play

Twelfth Night opens with a revealing pun. A servant asks Orsino, a love-struck duke, "Will you go hunt, my lord?" The servant wants to know if Orsino would like to hunt "the hart," or stag. But Orsino plays with the word by answering as if it meant "heart," and thus turns their conversation back to the subject of love.

Orsino is right: *Twelfth Night* is all about "hunting the heart." The comedy arises because the characters are not very skilled hunters. For most of the play, they can't quite track love down. It eludes their aim, but all the while it pursues them mercilessly. Love's in control, not the hunters who seek it. In the end, they never really do "catch" their desires. Instead, love comes out of hiding at last to set their confusion right.

All this takes place in Illyria, Orsino's dukedom. Technically, the name refers to a real region, an area that's part of the Balkan peninsula. But the Illyria of *Twelfth Night* is a head-over-heels land of fantasy, where everyone seems to be at least a touch mad. Love, in this play, comes dangerously close to delusion. Orsino believes he loves Olivia. But, as many readers have observed, he really seems most carried away by the *idea* of being in love. Olivia arrogantly thinks she can lock away her heart, then falls hopelessly for a woman disguised as a man. Sebastian cheerfully marries a woman who clearly imagines that he is someone else. Malvolio and Sir Andrew Aguecheek are tricked into hopelessly pursuing Olivia.

It soon becomes clear that Illyria's wisest head may belong to Feste, a professional fool. Among all the would-be lovers, only the heroine, Viola, sees things clearly. Yet she too is trapped in an illusion, for she is trapped in her male disguise. Nevertheless, her intelligence about others and her clear knowledge of her own heart are richly rewarded in the end.

Twelfth Night's happy ending has a dark undertone. The effect is both powerful and slightly puzzling. The comedy's distinctively moody tone looks forward to Shakespeare's "romances"—mysterious, magical plays like *The Tempest* and *A Winter's Tale*. Some scholars have even

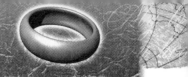

considered *Twelfth Night* a kind of "farewell to comedy" for Shakespeare. For these scholars, *Twelfth Night* (c. 1601) shows signs of Shakespeare's desire to explore the darker sides of human nature. They note that *Twelfth Night* was probably written just before Shakespeare began writing the tragedies of human evil that began with *Hamlet*.

Twelfth Night's dark side rests mainly on its subplot, involving an extended trick played on Olivia's steward, Malvolio. Malvolio is certainly a comic villain. He is a pompous killjoy whose character represents a threat to the very spirit of love, comedy, and art, the spirit that infuses the play. On the other hand, Malvolio has very little power over some characters in the play, but they plot out the joke anyway. This is especially true of one of his tormentors, Sir Toby, an amusing man who is also a drunken parasite. As the hoax against Malvolio plays on from act to act, many playgoers may begin to feel that the joke wears thin. The hoaxers' justified revenge begins to seem like unnecessary punishment. Malvolio's angry exit from the play darkens its last act— as do some other notes of violence and Feste's worldly-wise final song.

The effect is to make the traditional sunny outcome that is here, as always, the essential requirement for a comedy feel oddly fragile. We can't forget that "happy endings" on stage are perfected by art, not life. They rarely resemble the mixed, confusing outcomes of our existence in real time. However, this is also why comic endings are so pleasing. *Twelfth Night* shows the triumph of love over sorrow. As Viola, Orsino, Olivia, and Sebastian make their final exits into the world where "they all lived happily ever after," Feste's song requests richly deserved applause. As Feste tells us, "the rain it raineth every day." *Twelfth Night* lets us come out of that rain—for although the cold world may wait outside, we can still warm ourselves with the comforts of Shakespeare's comedy.

Twelfth Night's Sources

No battles take place in *Twelfth Night*. Even the traditional "battle of the sexes" in this romantic comedy is confused, since the heroine is disguised as a boy throughout. Nevertheless, Shakespeare actually borrowed *Twelfth Night*'s plot from the tales of a retired military man.

Shakespeare's primary source for *Twelfth Night* seems to have been a story by one Barnabe Rich (also spelled Barnaby Riche), who was an ex-soldier and writer on military affairs. Rich turned to lighter topics when he published a collection of tales called *Riche his Farewelle to*

Militarie Profession in 1581. The collection included the story of
"Apolonius and Silla," which appears to have been Shakespeare's model
for the romantic mixups among *Twelfth Night*'s Orsino, Viola, Olivia,
and Sebastian. In Rich's version, the young noblewoman Silla disguises
herself as a male page, "Silvio," and works in the household of the man
she loves. In his service she woos another woman, who soon falls in
love with "Silvio." As in *Twelfth Night,* the pairs are finally sorted out
after Silla's brother arrives on the scene.

Rich did not invent this web of relationships all by himself.
Scholars have traced the story's origins to an Italian play of the 1530s
called *Gl'Ingannati* ("The Deceived Ones") by an unknown author.
The play spawned prose spin-off versions by another Italian writer,
Matteo Bandello, and by the French writer François Belleforest.
Belleforest's version (1570) was probably the source that Rich used for
the tale. Shakespeare knew both Bandello's and Belleforest's collections
of romantic tales, and it is possible that he may have been familiar with
Gl'Ingannati as well. But this cannot be proven, and most Shakespeare
experts assume that Rich was the most likely source for *Twelfth Night's*
main plot.

Shakespeare was also inspired by his own earlier plays as he wrote
this charming comedy. The heroines of *As You Like It* (c. 1599), *The
Merchant of Venice* (c. 1596–1598), and *The Two Gentlemen of Verona*
(c. 1590–1595) all disguise themselves as men for a portion of each
play. (Shakespeare enjoyed the comic irony of a *boy* playing a *girl* playing a *boy*.) In *Two Gentlemen,* the character Julia disguises herself as
her true love's male servant. In the process, she is forced to carry his
messages to another woman.

The Text of *Twelfth Night*

Twelfth Night was first printed in the First Folio of 1623. Most scholars
believe that this version is based on a scribe's transcription of
Shakespeare's own hand-written manuscript, as copied either for the
First Folio's editors or for the use of Shakespeare's own acting company. All modern editions of the play are based on the First Folio text,
although there may be slight variations among them based on individual editorial decisions.

The earliest reference to a performance of *Twelfth Night* appears in
an audience member's diary entry from 1602. Scholars believe the play
was written earlier than that, however. It has been suggested that

Twelfth Night was written for a special performance before Queen Elizabeth on January 6, 1601—the actual date of the Twelfth Night holiday. On that occasion, the Queen's special guest was an Italian nobleman named Orsino. Although this theory is undeniably attractive, most scholars now think it is unlikely and date the play's composition no earlier than mid-1601.

Twelfth Night

Original text and modern version

Characters

Orsino   the duke of Illyria

Viola   Sebastian's sister, also called Cesario

Olivia   a rich countess loved by Orsino

Sir Toby Belch   Olivia's uncle

Sir Andrew Aguecheek   friend of Sir Toby

Maria   Olivia's maid

Malvolio   Olivia's steward

Feste   a fool

Sebastian   Viola's brother

Antonio   a sea captain, friend of Sebastian

Fabian   a servant and fool

Valentine
Curio   } gentlemen that serve the duke

A Sea Captain   Viola's friend

Lords, Priests, Sailors, Officers, Musicians, and other **Attendants**

All the World's a Stage Introduction

Twelfth Night! Shakespeare's audience knew that this special celebration, which fell 12 days after Christmas, ended the holiday season. It was time for one last party before life returned to normal. Why did Shakespeare pick this name? Most critics think he was signaling that this play is full of carnival spirit, with costumes, pretense, and instant love.

The merriment takes place in Illyria, a region on the east coast of the Adriatic Sea where pirates were supposed to hide out. It had come to represent a place that was "not of this world." In Illyria, love, not logic or power, rules.

The subtitle of the play, *What You Will,* means about the same as today's "whatever…." But for Elizabethans, *will* had to do with intense—and irrational—love and desire. The phrase tells us this story is not terribly serious. Make of it whatever you will.

What's in a Name? Characters

Into this world comes Viola, a young woman who is shipwrecked. Believing her twin brother has drowned, she finds an ingenious way to protect herself. Watch for a change in Viola's name and role.

Illyria's ruler is Duke Orsino, who is obsessed with Countess Olivia. However, because of the deaths of her father and, more recently, her brother, Olivia has decided to mourn for seven years. Her plans do not include Orsino.

Sir Toby Belch is Olivia's uncle. (His name is a pun on his appetite.) He and his dim-witted friend, Sir Andrew Aguecheek, like to dance, eat, and drink. (*Aguecheek* is a pun on a disease called *ague,* possibly malaria. A person with ague probably had a pasty yellow complexion and was thin and spindly.) Toby also loves to flirt with Olivia's witty maid, Maria.

Malvolio, Olivia's steward, runs her estate. The differences between him and the other characters in *Twelfth Night* are the basis for the play's humor.

Finally, there is Feste, a wise and witty fool. Because a fool could be blunt and honest, pay attention to Feste's comments.

COME WHAT MAY Things to Watch For

The very first speech of *Twelfth Night* tells you about a theme that runs throughout the play. "If music be the food of love, play on," says Duke Orsino. In Illyria, everyone is focused on love. It may be love between family members, men and women, or for an idea, such as power. But be skeptical. That love can be real, bursting upon a character in a moment. Or it may be *fancy*—being in love with love. And remember, this is carnival.

All Our Yesterdays **Historical and Social Context**

In Shakespeare's time people believed that astrology determined a person's physical and emotional health. A person whose sign was Cancer (June 22–July 22) would be ruled by the heart, the seat of love. A person whose sign was Scorpio (October 23–November 21) was ruled by the liver, the seat of the emotions. The stomach was the seat of courage, and the spleen the source of anger. Duke Orsino says that Olivia's liver, brain, and heart (i.e., emotions, reason, and love) are all ruled by her brother's death.

Tied in with the influence of astrology were the *humours,* or bodily "fluids." There were four: choler (yellow bile), blood, phlegm, and melancholy (black bile). An overabundance of any particular fluid affected a person's personality and physical nature. For instance, someone ruled by choler would be angry and temperamental and would be physically hot and "dry."

Now we don't believe in humours, but we've kept some of the terms. Then, a *sanguine* person was ruled by blood and was jolly and lusty. Today, a sanguine person is confident and optimistic. Then, a *phlegmatic* person was sluggish and slow. Today, a phlegmatic person is slow-moving or passive.

The Play's the Thing **Staging**

Much of Act I takes place at Olivia's house, with scenes in the "upstairs" formal world of love and the raucous "downstairs" world of drink, dance, and private jokes. "Upstairs love" is discussed in terms of ideals and emotions, "downstairs love" in terms of sexuality.

Staging the play also depends on conventions, or accepted practices. Elizabethan stories often included such things as pirates, shipwrecks, and disguises. When fantastic things happened on stage and the characters didn't seem to notice, theatergoers went along as well.

My Words Fly Up **Language**

Viola, Olivia, Malvolio. Shakespeare probably selected such similar names for a reason. To figure out why, pay particular attention to these three characters. Keep in mind that in Latin *vol-* means "will" or "wish." It can also indicate inclination or desire.

In Scene 1, Orsino's friend Curio asks the duke to go hunting for a *hart,* or deer. Orsino replies with a pun: He's already hunting for his *heart,* which Olivia has captured. Orsino then compares his situation with the Greek myth of Actaeon. While out hunting, by accident Actaeon saw the goddess Artemis bathing in a pool. To punish him, she turned him into a deer. His hunting dogs then chased him down and killed him. Orsino is saying that his love and desires have turned upon him. His great passion is tearing him apart.

Act I

Scene I

The Duke's Palace. Enter **Duke, Curio, Lords, Musicians**
attending.

Duke   If music be the food of love, play on;
Give me excess of it, that, surfeiting,
The appetite may sicken, and so die.
That strain again! It had a dying fall;
5   O, it came o'er my ear like the sweet sound
That breathes upon a bank of violets,
Stealing and giving odour. Enough! no more;
'Tis not so sweet now as it was before.
O spirit of love! how quick and fresh art thou,
10   That, notwithstanding thy capacity
Receiveth as the sea, nought enters there,
Of what validity and pitch soe'er,
But falls into abatement and low price,
Even in a minute; so full of shapes is fancy
15   That it alone is high fantastical.

Curio   Will you go hunt, my lord?

Duke   What, Curio?

Curio   The hart.

Duke   Why, so I do, the noblest that I have.
20   O, when mine eyes did see Olivia first,
Methought she purged the air of pestilence;
That instant was I turned into a hart,

Duke Orsino's palace in Illyria. The **Duke, Curio,** *other* **Lords,** *and* **Musicians** *enter.*

— Metaphor

Duke [*to* **Musicians**] If music is love's food, play on. Give me too much of it, so that my appetite, overfed, gets so sick of music that it dies. Play that part again! It had a sad sound. Oh, to my ear it was like the sweet sound of a breeze passing over a violet-covered hillside, taking and bringing odors. That's enough, no more of it. It's not so sweet as it was before. Oh spirit of love, how keen and hungry you are! In spite of having as huge a capacity as the sea, nothing comes to you, no matter how valuable or great it is, but it becomes small and worthless in a single moment! Love is so wildly varied that nothing else can measure up to it.

– Simile

Curio Will you go hunting, my lord?

Duke What?

Curio The deer.

Duke Why, that's what I'm doing. [*Places his hand on his heart*] With the dearest thing in me. Oh, when my eyes first saw Olivia, I thought she purified the air. In that instant, I was turned into a deer, and my desires, fierce and cruel hounds,

– Don't judge a book by its cover

And my desires, like fell and cruel hounds,
E'er since pursue me.

[*Enter* **Valentine**]

25   How now! What news from her?

Valentine   So please my lord, I might not be admitted;
But from her handmaid do return this answer;
Simile   The element itself, till seven years' heat,
Shall not behold her face at ample view;
30   But, like a cloistress, she will veiled walk,
And water once a day her chamber round
With eye-offending brine; all this to season
A brother's dead love, which she would keep fresh
And lasting in her sad remembrance.

35   **Duke**   O, she that hath a heart of that fine frame
To pay this debt of love but to a brother,
How will she love, when the rich golden shaft
Hath killed the flock of all affections else
That live in her; when liver, brain, and heart,
40   These sovereign thrones, are all supplied, and filled
Her sweet perfections, with one self king!
Away before me to sweet beds of flowers;   *Rhyme*
Love-thoughts lie rich when canopied with bowers.

[*Exeunt*]

have pursued me ever since. [**Valentine** *enters*] Well, what did she say?

Valentine My lord, I wasn't allowed to see her. But from her handmaid I brought back this answer: The sky itself shall not see her face uncovered until seven summers have passed. But like a nun behind walls, she will walk round her room wearing a veil, and weeping salty tears. All this she does to preserve her love for her dead brother, which she wants to keep fresh and lasting in her sad memory.

Duke Oh, her heart is so tender that she does all this out of love for just a brother. How will she love when Cupid's golden arrow has killed all other affections in her? When passion, thought, and emotion—separate kingdoms within her—are all ruled by one lord who is the sole object of her sweet, perfect love? Lead me to sweet beds of flowers. Thinking of love is rich when under the trees.

[*They exit*]

Act I

Scene II

The Sea-coast. Enter **Viola, a Captain** *and* **Sailors.**

Viola What country, friends, is this?

Captain   This is Illyria, lady.

Viola And what should I do in Illyria?
My brother he is in Elysium:
5   Perchance he is not drowned; what think you, sailors?

Captain It is perchance that you yourself were saved.

For-
shadowing **Viola** O, my poor brother! And so perchance may he be. (He may be alive)

Captain True, madam; and, to comfort you with chance,
Assure yourself, after our ship did split,
10   When you and those poor number saved with you
Hung on our driving boat, I saw your brother,
Most provident in peril, bind himself,
Courage and hope both teaching him the practice,
To a strong mast that lived upon the sea;
15   Where, like Arion on the dolphin's back,
I saw him hold acquaintance with the waves
So long as I could see.

Viola For saying so, there's gold;
Mine own escape unfoldeth to my hope,
20   Whereto thy speech serves for authority,
The like of him. Know'st thou this country?

The seacoast of Illyria. **Viola,** *a* **Sea Captain,** *and some* **Sailors** *enter. They are survivors of a shipwreck.*

Viola What is this country, friends?

Captain This is Illyria, my lady.

Viola What am I doing in Illyria? My brother is in heaven. Perhaps he is not drowned. What do you think, sailors?

Captain It was only by good fortune that you yourself were saved.

Viola Oh, my poor brother! Perhaps he may be too.

Captain True, madam, and to comfort you with a hopeful chance, let me assure you of something. After our ship began to sink, when you and those few others saved with you clung to our drifting boat, I saw your brother. Very resourceful in the face of danger, he tied himself to a sturdy mast that floated on the water, courage and hope both encouraging him in the action. For as long as I could see him, I watched him there, battling the waves like Arion, the ancient poet in Greek myth, who saved himself by riding on a dolphin's back.

Viola [*giving him money*] For telling me that, here's gold. My own escape makes me hope he may have also, and your story supports this. Do you know this country?

Captain Ay, madam, well; for I was bred and born
Not three hours' travel from this very place.

Viola Who governs here?

25 **Captain** A noble duke, in nature as in name.

~Duke
(Reputation and
(really kind)
good

Viola What is his name?

Captain Orsino.

Viola Orsino! I have heard my father name him;
He was a bachelor then.

30 **Captain** And so is now, or was so very late;
For but a month ago I went from hence,
And then 'twas fresh in murmur – as, you know,
What great ones do the less will prattle of –
That he did seek the love of fair Olivia.

35 **Viola** What's she?

~Oliva

Captain A virtuous maid, the daughter of a count
That died some twelvemonth since, then leaving her
In the protection of his son, her brother,
Who shortly also died; for whose dear love,
40 They say, she hath abjured the company
And sight of men.

Viola   O that I served that lady,
And might not be delivered to the world
Till I had made mine own occasion mellow,
45 What my estate is!

Captain   That were hard to compass,
Because she will admit no kind of suit,
No, not the duke's.

Viola There is a fair behaviour in thee, captain;
50 And though that nature with a beauteous wall
Doth oft close in pollution, yet of thee
I will believe thou hast a mind that suits

Captain Yes, madam, I know it well, for I was born and raised not three hours' travel from this very place.

Viola Who governs here?

Captain A noble duke, both in birth and character.

Viola What is his name?

Captain Orsino.

Viola Orsino! I have heard my father speak of him. He was a bachelor then.

Captain And he is one now, or was very recently. For I left here only a month ago, and then it was freshly rumored—as you know, ordinary people will gossip about nobility—that he sought the love of the fair Olivia.

Viola Who is she?

Captain A virtuous maiden, the daughter of a count who died some twelve months ago. He left her under the protection of his son, her brother, who shortly afterward also died. Because of the dear love she had for her brother, people say, she has given up the sight and company of men.

Viola Oh, I wish that I could serve that lady, and that my situation might remain hidden from the world until I was better prepared to reveal it!

not what always they seem

Captain That would be difficult to accomplish, because she will not grant anyone's desire to see her, not even the duke's.

Viola You seem a decent man, Captain. And though nature will often enclose foulness behind a handsome front, yet I will believe that you have a mind that matches your pleasing

With this thy fair and outward character.
I prithee, and I'll pay thee bounteously,
55   Conceal me what I am, and be my aid
For such disguise as haply shall become
The form of my intent. I'll serve this duke;
Thou shalt present me as an eunuch to him;
It may be worth thy pains; for I can sing
60   And speak to him in many sorts of music
That will allow me very worth his service.
What else may hap, to time I will commit;
Only shape thou thy silence to my wit.

Captain Be you his eunuch, and your mute I'll be;
65   When my tongue blabs, then let mine eyes not see.

Viola I thank thee; lead me on.

[Exeunt]

appearance. Please help me—for which I'll pay you generously—to conceal myself, and assist me in a disguise that may suit my purpose. I'll serve this duke. You shall present me to him as a eunuch. It will be worth your trouble, for I can sing and perform for him many kinds of music that will make me a valuable servant to him. What else may happen, only time will tell. Just keep quiet about my plan.

Captain You be his eunuch, and I'll keep quiet for you; when my tongue blabs, may I go blind.

Viola I thank you. Lead on.

[*They exit*]

Act I

Scene III

Olivia's House. Enter **Sir Toby Belch** *and* **Maria.**

Sir Toby What a plague means my niece, to take the death of her brother thus? I am sure care's an enemy to life.

Maria By my troth, Sir Toby, you must come in earlier o' nights; your cousin, my lady, takes great exceptions to your
5   ill hours.

Sir Toby Why, let her except before excepted.

Maria Ay, but you must confine yourself within the modest limits of order.

Sir Toby Confine? I'll confine myself no finer than I am.
10   These clothes are good enough to drink in, and so be these boots too; an they be not, let them hang themselves in their own straps.

Maria That quaffing and drinking will undo you; I heard my lady talk of it yesterday; and of a foolish knight that you
15   brought in one night here to be her wooer.

Sir Toby Who? Sir Andrew Aguecheek?

Maria Ay, he.

Sir Toby He's as tall a man as any's in Illyria.

Maria What's that to the purpose?

20 **Sir Toby** Why, he has three thousand ducats a year.

A room in Olivia's house. Her kinsman **Sir Toby Belch** *and her maid* **Maria** *enter.*

Sir Toby What the devil does my niece mean by taking her brother's death in this way? I am sure that worrying is unhealthy.

Maria By my faith, Sir Toby, you must come in earlier at night. Your kinswoman, my lady, takes great exception to your late hours.

Sir Toby Well, let her except me from her exceptions.

Maria Yes, but you must confine yourself within the limits of what's proper.

Sir Toby Confine? I'll confine myself no more properly than the finery I'm in. These clothes are good enough to drink in, and so are these boots too. If they're not, let them hang themselves in their own straps.

Maria This heavy drinking will ruin you. I heard my lady talk of it yesterday, and of a foolish knight that you brought here one night to woo her.

Sir Toby Who, Sir Andrew Aguecheek?

Maria Yes, him.

Sir Toby He is the equal of any man in Illyria.

Maria In what way?

Sir Toby Why, his income is three thousand ducats a year.

Maria Ay, but he'll have but a year in all these ducats; he's a very fool and a prodigal.

Sir Toby Fie, that you'll say so! He plays o' the viol-de-gamboys, and speaks three or four languages word for word
25 without book, and hath all the good gifts of nature.

Maria He hath indeed, almost natural; for besides that he's a fool, he's a great quarreller; and but that he hath the gift of a coward to allay the gust he hath in quarrelling, 'tis thought among the prudent he would quickly have the gift of a
30 grave.

Sir Toby By this hand, they are scoundrels and substractors that say so of him. Who are they?

Maria They that add, moreover, he's drunk nightly in your company.

35 **Sir Toby** With drinking healths to my niece. I'll drink to her as long as there is a passage in my throat and drink in Illyria. He's a coward and a coystril that will not drink to my niece till his brains turn o' the toe like a parish-top. What, wench! Castiliano vulgo! for here comes Sir Andrew Agueface.

[*Enter* **Sir Andrew Aguecheek**]

40 **Sir Andrew** Sir Toby Belch! How now, Sir Toby Belch!

Sir Toby Sweet Sir Andrew!

Sir Andrew Bless you, fair shrew.

Maria And you too, sir.

Sir Toby Accost, Sir Andrew, accost.

45 **Sir Andrew** What's that?

Sir Toby My niece's chambermaid.

Maria Yes, but he will have spent all his ducats within one year. He's a complete fool and a spendthrift.

Sir Toby Shame on you for saying so! He plays the cello, and speaks three or four languages word for word by heart, and has all of nature's best gifts.

Maria He has indeed, like a natural-born idiot. Besides being a fool, he is a great quarreler, and—if he didn't have the gift of cowardice to lessen his enthusiasm for quarreling—it is thought by the wise that he would quickly have the gift of a grave.

Sir Toby [*raising his hand*] By this hand, they are scoundrels and subtractors [*He means "detractors"*] that say that about him. Who are they?

Maria Those who also say that he's drunk every night in your company.

Sir Toby With drinking toasts to my niece! I'll drink to her as long as there is a passage in my throat and drink in Illyria. He's a coward and a lowlife that will not drink to my niece till his brains spin like a top. What, girl? Speak of the devil! Here comes Sir Andrew Agueface.

[**Sir Andrew Aguecheek** *enters*]

Sir Andrew Sir Toby Belch! How goes it, Sir Toby?

Sir Toby Sweet Sir Andrew!

Sir Andrew [*to Maria*] Bless you, pretty little shrew.

Maria And you too, sir.

Sir Toby Accost her, Sir Andrew, accost her.

Sir Andrew Who's she?

Sir Toby My niece's chambermaid.

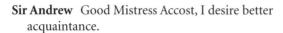

Sir Andrew Good Mistress Accost, I desire better
acquaintance.

Maria My name is Mary, sir.

50 **Sir Andrew** Good Mistress Mary Accost –

Sir Toby You mistake, knight; 'accost' is front her, board her,
woo her, assail her.

Sir Andrew By my troth, I would not undertake her in this
company. Is that the meaning of 'accost'?

55 **Maria** Fare you well, gentlemen.

Sir Toby An thou let part so, Sir Andrew, would thou
might'st never draw sword again!

Sir Andrew An you part so, mistress, I would I might never
draw sword again. Fair lady, do you think you have fools in
60 hand?

Maria Sir, I have not you by the hand.

Sir Andrew Marry, but you shall have; and here's my hand.

Maria Now, sir, 'thought is free'; I pray you, bring your hand
to the buttery-bar and let it drink.

65 **Sir Andrew** Wherefore, sweetheart? What's your metaphor?

Maria It's dry, sir.

Sir Andrew Why, I think so; I am not such an ass but I can
keep my hand dry. But what's your jest?

Maria A dry jest, sir.

70 **Sir Andrew** Are you full of them?

Maria Ay, sir, I have them at my fingers' ends; marry, now I
let go your hand, I am barren.

[*Exit*]

Sir Andrew   Good Mistress Accost, I would like to know you better.

Maria   My name is Mary, sir.

Sir Andrew   Good Mistress Mary Accost—

Sir Toby   You're mistaken, knight. "Accost" means make advances to her, take hold of her, woo her, grab her.

Sir Andrew   By my faith, I couldn't do that with people around. Is that the meaning of "accost"?

Maria   [*starting to leave*] Farewell, gentlemen.

Sir Toby   If you let her go like that, Sir Andrew, may you never draw your sword again.

Sir Andrew   If you go like that, madam, may I never draw my sword again. Fair lady, do you think you have fools in hand?

Maria   Sir, I don't have you by the hand.

Sir Andrew   Indeed, but you will have. [*Giving her his hand*] Here's my hand.

Maria   Well, sir, I may think what I like. Bring your hand to the pantry and let it drink.

Sir Andrew   What, sweetheart? What's your point?

Maria   It's dry, sir.

Sir Andrew   I should think so. I'm not such a fool that I can't keep my hand dry. But what's your joke?

Maria   A dry joke, sir.

Sir Andrew   Are you full of them?

Maria   Yes, sir. I have them at my fingertips. [*She lets go of his hand*] But indeed, now that I let your hand go, I have none.

[**Maria** *exits*]

Sir Toby O knight! thou lackest a cup of canary; when did I
see thee so put down?

75 **Sir Andrew** Never in your life, I think; unless you see canary
put me down. Methinks sometimes I have no more wit than
a Christian or an ordinary man has; but I am a great eater of
beef, and I believe that does harm to my wit.

Sir Toby No question.

80 **Sir Andrew** An I thought that, I'd forswear it. I'll ride home
tomorrow, Sir Toby.

Sir Toby Pourquoi, my dear knight?

Sir Andrew What is 'pourquoi'? Do or not do? I would I had
bestowed that time in the tongues that I have in fencing,
85 dancing, and bear-baiting. Oh, had I but followed the arts!

Sir Toby Then hadst thou had an excellent head of hair.

Sir Andrew Why, would that have mended my hair?

Sir Toby Past question; for thou seest it will not curl by
nature.

90 **Sir Andrew** But it becomes me well enough, does it not?

Sir Toby Excellent; it hangs like flax on a distaff, and I hope
to see a housewife take thee between her legs, and spin it off.

Sir Andrew Faith, I'll home tomorrow, Sir Toby; your niece
will not be seen; or if she be, it's four to one she'll none of
95 me. The count himself here hard by woos her.

Sir Toby She'll none o' the count; she'll not match above her
degree, neither in estate, years, nor wit; I have heard her
swear it. Tut, there's life in't, man.

Sir Toby   Oh, knight, you need a cup of wine! When did I ever see you so put down?

Sir Andrew   Never in your life, I think, unless you've seen wine put me down. Sometimes I think that I have no more brains than any Christian or ordinary man has. But I am a great eater of beef, and I believe that that does great harm to my wits.

Sir Toby   No question about it.

Sir Andrew   If I thought that, I'd give it up. [*Pause*] I'll ride home tomorrow, Sir Toby.

Sir Toby   [*using French for "why"*] Pourquoi, my dear knight?

Sir Andrew   What is *pourquoi?* Do or not do? I wish I had spent as much time learning foreign tongues as I have fencing, dancing, and bear-baiting. Oh, if I only I had followed the arts!

Sir Toby   Then you would have had an excellent head of hair. [*Punning on* tongues *and curling* tongs]

Sir Andrew   Why, would the arts have improved my hair?

Sir Toby   No question about it, for you see it will not curl by nature.

Sir Andrew   But it suits me well enough, doesn't it?

Sir Toby   Excellently. It hangs as limply as flax on a spindle. And I hope to see a housewife take you between her legs, and spin it off!

Sir Andrew   Truly, I'm going home tomorrow, Sir Toby. I can't get to see your niece. And if I do, it's four to one she'll have nothing to do with me. The count who lives near here woos her himself.

Sir Toby   She'll have nothing to do with the count. She'll not marry above her level, either in class, age, or intelligence. I have heard her swear it. Nonsense, you still have a chance, man!

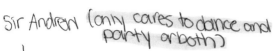

Sir Andrew (only cares to dance and party or both?)

Sir Andrew I'll stay a month longer. I am a fellow o' the
100   strangest mind i' the world; I delight in masques and revels
sometimes altogether.

Sir Toby Art thou good at these kickshawses, knight?

Sir Andrew As any man in Illyria, whatsoever he be, under
the degree of my betters; and yet I will not compare with an
105   old man.

Sir Toby What is thy excellence in a galliard, knight?

Sir Andrew Faith, I can cut a caper.

Sir Toby And I can cut the mutton to 't.

Sir Andrew And I think I have the back-trick simply as
110   strong as any man in Illyria.

Sir Toby Wherefore are these things hid? Wherefore have
these gifts a curtain before 'em? Are they like to take dust,
like Mistress Mall's picture? Why dost thou not go to church
in a galliard, and come home in a coranto? My very walk
115   should be a jig; I would not so much as make water but in a
sink-a-pace. What dost thou mean? Is it a world to hide virtues in? I did think, by the excellent constitution of thy leg,
it was formed under the star of a galliard.

Sir Andrew Ay, 'tis strong, and it does indifferent well in a
120   flame-coloured stock. Shall we set about some revels?

Sir Toby What shall we do else? Were we not born under
Taurus?

Sir Andrew Taurus! that's sides and heart.

Sir Toby No, sir, it is legs and thighs. Let me see thee caper.
125   Ha! higher; ha, ha! excellent!

[Exeunt]

Sir Andrew I'll stay a month longer. I'm a fellow with the oddest mind in the world. Sometimes all I care for is dances and merrymaking.

Sir Toby Are you good at these trifles, knight?

Sir Andrew As good as any man in Illyria, whoever he is, except those who are better than me. But I'm not as good as an experienced man.

Sir Toby How good are you at dancing a jig, knight?

Sir Andrew Truly, I can cut a caper.

Sir Toby And I can cut the mutton to go with it. [*Punning on two meanings of* caper, *"lively leap" and "pickle"*]

Sir Andrew And I can do the backward step as well as any man in Illyria.

Sir Toby Why do you hide these things? Why do these talents have a curtain in front of them? Are they going to get dusty, like a family portrait? Why do you not dance to church and home again? If I were you, I wouldn't walk, but jig. I would even dance to the bathroom. What were you thinking of? Is this a world to hide talents in? I did think, judging by the excellent shape of your legs, that you were born to dance.

Sir Andrew Yes, they're strong. And they do look pretty good in bright orange stockings. Shall we try some dances?

Sir Toby What else would we do? Were we not born under the sign of Taurus?

Sir Andrew Taurus? Doesn't that influence sides and heart?

Sir Toby No, sir, it's legs and thighs. Let me see you leap. [**Sir Andrew** *leaps*] Ha, higher! Ha, ha, excellent!

[**Sir Toby** *and* **Sir Andrew** *exit*]

Act I
Scene IV

The Duke's Palace. Enter **Valentine,** *and* **Viola** *in man's attire.*

Valentine If the duke continue these favours towards you, Cesario, you are like to be much advanced: he hath known you but three days and already you are no stranger.

Viola You either fear his humour or my negligence, that you
5   call in question the continuance of his love. Is he inconstant, sir, in his favours?

Valentine No, believe me.

Viola I thank you. Here comes the count.

[*Enter* **Duke, Curio** *and* **Attendants**]

Duke Who saw Cesario, ho?

10 **Viola** On your attendance, my lord; here.

Duke Stand you awhile aloof. Cesario,
      Thou know'st no less but all; I have unclasped
      To thee the book even of my secret soul.
      Therefore, good youth, address thy gait unto her;
15   Be not denied access, stand at her doors,
      And tell them, there thy fixed foot shall grow
      Till thou have audience.

A room in Duke Orsino's palace. **Valentine** *enters with* **Viola,** *who is now dressed as a man and is known as* **Cesario.**

Valentine If the duke continues to favor you, Cesario, you are likely to get promoted. He has only known you three days, and already you have become close to him.

Viola If you doubt that his love will continue, you must fear either his moods or my neglectfulness. Is he fickle, sir, in his favors?

Valentine No, believe me.

Viola I thank you. Here comes the duke.

[*The* **Duke, Curio,** *and* **Attendants** *enter*]

Duke Who has seen Cesario?

Viola Here, my lord, at your service.

Duke [*to* **Attendants**] Stand aside for a little while. [*To* **Viola**] Cesario, you know everything about me. Even my soul's secrets are an open book to you. Therefore, good lad, go to her. Don't be denied access. Stand at her door and tell her servants that your feet will take root there until you are allowed to see her.

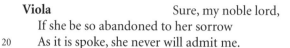

Viola   Sure, my noble lord,
   If she be so abandoned to her sorrow
20   As it is spoke, she never will admit me.

Duke   Be clamorous, and leap all civil bounds,
   Rather than make unprofited return.

Viola   Say I do speak with her, my lord; what then?

Duke   O! then unfold the passion of my love;
25   Surprise her with discourse of my dear faith;
   It shall become thee well to act my woes;
   She will attend it better in thy youth
   Than in a nuncio's of more grave aspect.

Viola   I think not so, my lord.

30 **Duke**   Dear lad, believe it;
   For they shall yet belie thy happy years
   That say thou art a man; Diana's lip
   Is not more smooth and rubious; thy small pipe
   Is as the maiden's organ, shrill and sound,
35   And all is semblative a woman's part.
   I know thy constellation is right apt
   For this affair. Some four or five attend him;
   All, if you will; for I myself am best
   When least in company. Prosper well in this,
40   And thou shalt live as freely as thy lord,
   To call his fortune thine.

Viola   I'll do my best
   To woo your lady. (*Aside*) Yet, a barful strife!
   Whoe'er I woo, myself would be his wife.

[*Exeunt*]

46

Viola Surely, my noble lord, if she is so completely wrapped up in her grief as people say, she will never see me.

Duke Be demanding and forget good manners rather than return unsuccessful.

Viola Say that I do speak with her, my lord, what then?

Duke Oh, then reveal the passion of my love. Overpower her with an account of my heartfelt devotion. It will be very suitable for you to present my sorrows. She will receive it better coming from someone young like you, rather than an older messenger.

Viola I don't think so, my lord.

Duke Dear lad, take my word for it. For those that would call you a man would be denying you this youthful time of life. The lips of the virgin goddess Diana are not smoother and more ruby-red than yours. Your small voice is like a girl's, high and clear. And, in general, you could pass for a woman. I know your nature is well suited to this business. [*To* **Attendants**] Four or five of you go with him. All of you, if you like, for I am at my best when most alone. [*To* **Viola**] Succeed well in this, and you shall live as richly as your lord, as though his fortune were yours.

Viola I'll do my best to woo your lady. [*To herself*] But this task has problems! Because whoever I woo, I would rather be his wife myself.

[*They exit*]

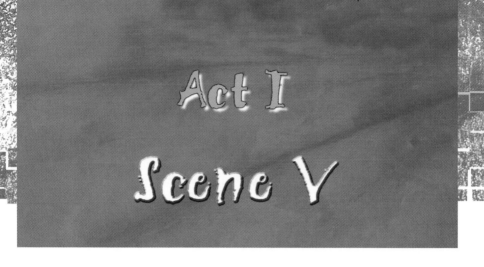

Act I

Scene V

Olivia's House. Enter **Maria** *and* **Feste,** *the clown.*

Maria Nay, either tell me where thou hast been, or I will not open my lips so wide as a bristle may enter in way of thy excuse. My lady will hang thee for thy absence.

Feste Let her hang me; he that is well hanged in this world
5 needs to fear no colours.

Maria Make that good.

Feste He shall see none to fear.

Maria A good lenten answer; I can tell thee where that saying was born, of 'I fear no colours'.

10 **Feste** Where, good Mistress Mary?

Maria In the wars; and that may you be bold to say in your foolery.

Feste Well, God give them wisdom that have it; and those that are fools, let them use their talents.

15 **Maria** Yet you will be hanged for being so long absent; or, to be turned away, is not that as good as a hanging to you?

Feste Many a good hanging prevents a bad marriage; and, for turning away, let summer bear it out.

A room in Olivia's house. **Maria** *and* **Feste,** *Olivia's clown (or jester), enter.*

Maria No; either tell me where you have been or I will not open my lips a hairsbreadth to make excuses for you. My lady will hang you for being absent.

Feste Let her hang me. He that is well hanged in this world need "fear no colors." [*Proverbial for "fear nothing" and punning on* collars, *"hangman's nooses"*]

Maria What do you mean by that?

Feste He shall see none to fear!

Maria A feeble answer. I can tell you the origin of the saying, "I fear no colors."

Feste Where, good Mistress Mary?

Maria In the wars. [*Here* colors *means "enemy flags"*] Be sure to use that in your jesting.

Feste Well, may God give wisdom to the wise. And those that are fools, let them use their abilities.

Maria You will be hanged for being absent so long. Or you'll be dismissed; for you, wouldn't that be just as bad as being hanged?

Feste Many a good hanging prevents a bad marriage. As for being dismissed, summer will make that easier.

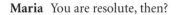

Maria You are resolute, then?

20 **Feste** Not so, neither; but I am resolved on two points.

Maria That if one break, the other will hold; or, if both
break, your gaskins fall.

Feste Apt, in good faith; very apt. Well, go thy way; if Sir
Toby would leave drinking, thou wert as witty a piece of
25 Eve's flesh as any in Illyria.

Maria Peace, you rogue, no more o' that. Here comes my
lady; make your excuse wisely, you were best.

[*Exit*]

Don't judge a book by its cover

Feste Wit, an't be thy will, put me into good fooling! Those
wits that think they have thee, do very oft prove fools; and I,
30 that am sure I lack thee, may pass for a wise man; for what
says Quinapalus? 'Better a witty fool than a foolish wit.'

[*Enter* **Olivia, Malvolio,** *and* **Attendants**]

Feste is the fool/ entertainer, but he's smart

God bless thee, lady!

Olivia Take the fool away.

Feste Do you not hear, fellows? Take away the lady.

35 **Olivia** Go to, you're a dry fool; I'll no more of you; besides
you grow dishonest.

Feste Two faults, madonna, that drink and good counsel will
amend; for give the dry fool drink, then is the fool not dry;
bid the dishonest man mend himself; if he mend, he is no
40 longer dishonest; if he cannot, let the botcher mend him.

Maria   You are completely determined, then?

Feste   No, I'm not; but I am resolved on two points.

Maria   [*punning on* points *meaning "laces used to hold up breeches"*]   That if one breaks, the other will hold; but if both break, your breeches fall down.

Feste   Apt, indeed. Very apt. Well, run along. If Sir Toby would give up drinking, you'd be as witty a daughter of our mother Eve as any young woman in Illyria.

Maria   Enough of that, you rogue. Here comes my lady. You'd be wise to come up with a clever excuse.

[**Maria** *exits*]

Feste   [*to himself*]   Wit, if it be your will, please make me funny! Those clever people that think that they have wit often prove to be fools. So I, that am sure have none, may pass for a wise man. For as Quinapulus [*Feste's invented authority*] says, "Better a witty fool than a foolish wit."

[**Olivia,** *her steward* **Malvolio,** *and* **Attendants** *enter*]

[*To* **Olivia**]   God bless you, lady!

Olivia   [*to* **Attendants**]   Take the fool away.

Feste   [*to* **Attendants**]   Didn't you hear her, you fellows? Take the lady away.

Olivia   [*to* **Feste**]   Enough! You're a dull fool. I want no more of you. Besides, you're growing dishonest.

Feste   Those are two faults, my lady, that can be mended with drink and good advice. For if you give drink to the dry fool, then he's no longer dry. Tell the dishonest man to mend his

Anything that's mended is but patched; virtue that
transgresses is but patched with sin; and sin that amends is
but patched with virtue. If that this simple syllogism will
serve, so; if it will not, what remedy? As there is no true
45   cuckold but calamity, so beauty's a flower. The lady bade
take away the fool; therefore, I say again, take her away.

Olivia Sir, I bade them take away you.

Feste Misprision in the highest degree! Lady, *cucullus non
facit monachum:* that's as much to say as I wear not motley in
50   my brain. Good madonna, give me leave to prove you a fool.

Olivia Can you do it?

Feste Dexteriously, good madonna.

Olivia Make your proof.

Feste I must catechize you for it, madonna; good my mouse of
55   virtue, answer me.

Olivia Well, sir, for want of other idleness, I'll bide your
proof.

Feste Good madonna, why mournest thou?

Olivia Good fool, for my brother's death.

60 **Feste** I think his soul is in hell, madonna.

Olivia I know his soul is in heaven, fool.

Feste The more fool, madonna, to mourn for your brother's
soul being in heaven. Take away the fool, gentlemen.

Olivia What think you of this fool, Malvolio? Doth he not
65   mend?

ways. If he does, then he is no longer dishonest. If he cannot, let the tailor mend him. Anything that's mended is only patched. Virtue that goes wrong is only patched with sin. Sin that mends its ways is only patched with virtue. If this simple reasoning convinces you, fine. If it doesn't, what more can I say? You won't remain faithful to your grief, because youth is fleeting. [*To* **Attendants**] The lady ordered you to take away the fool. Therefore, I say again: take her away.

Olivia Sir, I ordered them to take you away.

Feste A mistake of the highest order. Lady, "a hood does not make a monk." That is like saying that I don't wear a fool's cap and bells on my brain. My good lady, give me permission to prove you a fool.

Olivia Can you do it?

Feste Easily, my good lady.

Olivia Present your arguments.

Feste To do it, I must question you. My good, virtuous mouse, answer me.

Olivia Well, sir, for lack of other amusements, I will answer your questions.

Feste My good lady, why do you mourn?

Olivia Good fool, for my brother's death.

Feste I think his soul is in hell, my lady.

Olivia I know his soul is in heaven, fool.

Feste Then what a fool you are, my lady, to mourn for your brother's soul, which is in heaven. [*To* **Attendants**] Take away the fool, gentlemen.

Olivia What do you think of this fool, Malvolio? Doesn't he improve?

Malvolio Yes; and shall do till the pangs of death shake him;
infirmity, that decays the wise, doth ever make the better
fool.

70 **Feste** God send you, sir, a speedy infirmity, for the better
increasing your folly! Sir Toby will be sworn that I am no fox,
but he will not pass his word for two pence that you are no
fool.

Olivia How say you to that, Malvolio?

Malvolio I marvel your ladyship takes delight in such a
75 barren rascal; I saw him put down the other day with an
ordinary fool that has no more brain than a stone. Look you
now, he's out of his guard already; unless you laugh and
minister occasion to him, he is gagged. I protest, I take these
wise men, that crow so at these set kind of fools, no better
80 than the fools' zanies.

Olivia O, you are sick of self-love, Malvolio, and taste with a
distempered appetite. To be generous, guiltless, and of free
disposition, is to take those things for bird-bolts that you
deem cannon-bullets. There is no slander in an allowed fool,
85 though he do nothing but rail; nor no railing in a known
discreet man, though he do nothing but reprove.

Malvolio is obsessed with himself — selfish

Feste Now, Mercury endue thee with leasing, for thou
speakest well of fools!

[*Enter* **Maria**]

Maria Madam, there is at the gate a young gentleman much
90 desires to speak with you.

Olivia From the Count Orsino, is it?

Maria I know not, madam; 'tis a fair young man, and well
attended.

Malvolio Yes, and he will continue to do so, until the pains of death grip him. The feebleness of age, which makes wise men less wise, only makes fools more foolish.

Feste May God make you feeble right away, sir, to increase your folly! Sir Toby will swear that I'm not a clever fellow, but he wouldn't wager two cents that you aren't a fool.

Olivia What do you say to that, Malvolio?

Malvolio I am amazed that your ladyship takes delight in such a dull rascal. I saw him put down the other day by an ordinary fool who has no more brains than a stone. Look at him: he doesn't have a comeback now. Unless you laugh and encourage him, he's speechless. Really, I believe that these wise men that laugh so loudly at these predictable fools are no better than the fools' assistants.

Olivia Oh, self-love has made you sick, Malvolio, and given you an unhealthy outlook. To be noble, innocent, and tolerant means to see as tiny darts what you see as cannonballs. There is nothing insulting about a fool who is permitted to speak his mind, although he does nothing but ridicule; and no ridicule in a man known for good judgment, although he does nothing but criticize.

Feste May the trickster god Mercury make you a skillful liar, for you speak well of fools!

[**Maria** *enters*]

Maria There is a young gentleman at the gate who desires very much to speak with you.

Olivia Is he from the Count Orsino?

Maria I don't know, madam. He is a handsome young man, and has a number of attendants.

Olivia Who of my people hold him in delay?

95 **Maria** Sir Toby, madam, your kinsman.

Olivia Fetch him off, I pray you; he speaks nothing but madman. Fie on him!

[*Exit* **Maria**]

Go you, Malvolio; if it be a suit from the count, I am sick or not at home, what you will to dismiss it.

[*Exit* **Malvolio**]

100 Now you see, sir, how your fooling grows old, and people dislike it.

Feste Thou hast spoke for us, madonna, as if thy eldest son should be a fool; whose skull Jove cram with brains! for here he comes, one of thy kin has a most weak *pia mater*.

[*Enter* **Sir Toby Belch**]

105 **Olivia** By mine honour, half drunk! What is he at the gate, cousin?

Sir Toby A gentleman.

Olivia A gentleman! What gentleman?

Sir Toby 'Tis a gentleman here – a plague o' these pickle-
110 herring! How now, sot!

Feste Good Sir Toby!

Olivia Cousin, cousin, how have you come so early by this lethargy?

Sir Toby Lechery! I defy lechery. There's one at the gate.

115 **Olivia** Ay, marry; what is he?

Olivia Which one of my people is waiting with him?

Maria Your kinsman Sir Toby, madam.

Olivia Get Sir Toby away, please. He talks like a lunatic. Shame on him!

[**Maria** *exits*]

Malvolio, you go. If it's a proposal from the count, say I am sick, or not at home, or whatever you like, to get rid of it.

[**Malvolio** *exits*]

[*To* **Feste**] Now you see, sir, how your fooling grows tiresome, and people dislike it.

Feste You spoke up for us jesters, my lady, as if your eldest son were a fool. May heaven cram his skull with brains, for here comes one of your kinsmen with a very weak mind.

[**Sir Toby** *enters*]

Olivia My word, he's half drunk. [*To* **Sir Toby**] Who is the man at the gate, cousin?

Sir Toby A gentleman.

Olivia A gentleman? What gentleman?

Sir Toby There's a gentleman here—[*He belches*]. Blast these pickled herrings! [*To* **Feste**] Greetings, fool!

Feste Good Sir Toby.

Olivia [*to* **Sir Toby**] Cousin, cousin, how have you managed so early to have this dullness, this lethargy?

Sir Toby [*half-hearing*] Lechery! I defy lechery! [*Pause*] There's someone at the gate.

Olivia Yes, indeed. Who is he?

Sir Toby Let him be the devil, an he will, I care not; give me faith, say I. Well, it's all one.

[*Exit*]

Olivia What's a drunken man like, fool?

Feste Like a drowned man, a fool, and a madman; one
120 draught above heat makes him a fool, the second mads him, and a third drowns him.

Olivia Go thou and seek the crowner, and let him sit o' my coz; for he's in the third degree of drink, he's drowned; go, look after him.

125 **Feste** He is but mad yet, madonna; and the fool shall look to the madman.

[*Exit*]

[*Enter* **Malvolio**]

Malvolio Madam, yond young fellow swears he will speak with you. I told him you were sick; he takes on him to understand so much, and therefore comes to speak with you.
130 I told him you were asleep; he seems to have a foreknowledge of that too, and therefore comes to speak with you. What is to be said to him, lady? He's fortified against any denial.

Simile

Olivia Tell him he shall not speak with me.

Malvolio Has been told so; and he says he'll stand at your
135 door like a sheriff's post, and be the supporter to a bench, but he'll speak with you.

Olivia What kind o' man is he?

Malvolio Why, of mankind.

Olivia What manner of man?

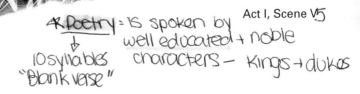

★ Poetry = is spoken by
well educated + noble
↓ characters — Kings + dukes
10 syllables
"Blank verse"

Sir Toby Let him be the devil if he likes, I don't care. Just give me faith, I say. Well, it doesn't matter. [*He leaves*]

★ Prose = is spoken by less well
educated characters,
(Full sentences) comedic characters,
or really emotional
characters.

Olivia What's a drunken man like, fool?

Feste Like a drowned man, a fool, and a madman. One drink too many makes him a fool, the second makes him mad, and the third drowns him.

Olivia You go and get the coroner, and let him examine my cousin. For he's in the third stage of drink; he's drowned. Go and take care of him.

Feste He is still only mad, my lady. And the fool shall look after the madman.

[**Feste** *exits*]

[**Malvolio** *enters*]

Malvolio Madam, the young fellow yonder swears he will speak with you. I told him you were sick. He claims to have known this, and for that very reason comes to speak with you. I told him you were asleep. He seems to have already known this, too, and for that reason comes to speak with you. What should I say to him lady? He has an answer to every excuse.

Olivia Tell him he shall not speak with me.

Malvolio He has been told so. And he says he'll stand at your door like a flagpole or hold up a bench, but he'll speak with you.

Olivia What kind of man is he?

Malvolio Why, just an ordinary man.

Olivia What manner of man?

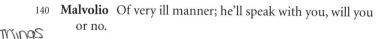

140 **Malvolio** Of very ill manner; he'll speak with you, will you or no.

Olivia Of what personage and years is he?

things are not always as they seem

Malvolio Not yet old enough for a man, nor young enough for a boy; as a squash is before 'tis a peascod, or a codling
145 when 'tis almost an apple; 'tis with him in standing water, between boy and man. He is very well-favoured, and he speaks very shrewishly; one would think his mother's milk were scarce out of him.

Olivia Let him approach. Call in my gentlewoman.

150 **Malvolio** Gentlewoman, my lady calls.

[*Exit*]

[*Enter* **Maria**]

Olivia Give me my veil; come, throw it o'er my face. We'll once more hear Orsino's embassy.

[*Enter* **Viola** *and* **Attendants**]

Viola The honourable lady of the house, which is she?

Olivia Speak to me; I shall answer for her. Your will?

155 **Viola** Most radiant, exquisite, and unmatchable beauty – I pray you, tell me if this be the lady of the house, for I never saw her. I would be loath to cast away my speech; for besides that it is excellently well penned, I have taken great pains to con it. Good beauties, let me sustain no scorn; I am very
160 comptible, even to the least sinister usage.

Olivia Whence came you, sir?

Viola I can say little more than I have studied, and that question's out of my part. Good gentle one, give me modest

Malvolio A very ill-mannered one. He'll speak with you, whether you want to or not.

Olivia What's he look like? How old is he?

Malvolio He is not yet old enough to be a man, nor young enough to be a boy. He's like an unripe peapod or a green apple. With him, the state between boy and man is like the still water at the turn of the tides. He is very handsome, and he speaks very sharply. One would think his mother had only recently stopped nursing him.

Olivia Let him come in. Call in my maid.

Malvolio Gentlewoman, my lady calls.

[**Malvolio** *exits*]

[**Maria** *enters*]

Olivia Give me my veil. Come, throw it over my face. We will once again hear Orsino's message.

[**Viola** *enters*]

Viola The honorable lady of the house, which is she?

Olivia Speak to me. I will answer for her. What do you want?

Viola [*beginning prepared speech*] Most radiant, exquisite, and unmatchable beauty— [*To* **Attendants**] Please tell me if this is the lady of the house, for I never saw her. I would hate to waste my speech. For in addition to its being very well written, I have taken a lot of trouble to learn it by heart. Lovely ladies, don't make fun of me. I am very sensitive, even to the slightest discourtesy.

Olivia Where did you come from, sir?

Viola I can say only what I have prepared, and that question is not in my speech. Good gentle one, give me reasonable

165 assurance if you be the lady of the house, that I may proceed in my speech.

Olivia Are you a comedian?

Viola No, my profound heart; and yet, by the very fangs of malice I swear I am not that I play. Are you the lady of the house?

170 **Olivia** If I do not usurp myself, I am.

Viola Most certain, if you are she, you do usurp yourself; for what is yours to bestow is not yours to reserve. But this is from my commission; I will on with my speech in your praise, and then show you the heart of my message.

175 **Olivia** Come to what is important in't; I forgive you the praise.

Viola Alas! I took great pains to study it, and 'tis poetical.

Olivia It is the more like to be feigned; I pray you keep it in. I heard you were saucy at my gates, and allowed your
180 approach, rather to wonder at you than to hear you. If you be not mad, be gone; if you have reason, be brief; 'tis not that time of moon with me to make one in so skipping a dialogue.

Maria Will you hoist sail, sir? here lies your way.

Viola No, good swabber; I am to hull here a little longer.
185 Some mollification for your giant, sweet lady.

Olivia Tell me your mind.

Viola I am a messenger.

Olivia Sure, you have some hideous matter to deliver, when the courtesy of it is so fearful. Speak your office.

assurance that you are the lady of the house, so that I may proceed with my speech.

Olivia Are you an actor?

Viola No, in all sincerity; and yet, despite wicked rumors, I swear I am not what I pretend to be. Are you the lady of the house?

Olivia Unless I do myself an injustice, I am.

Viola If you are the lady of the house, you are certainly doing yourself an injustice. For what is yours to give may not be yours to withhold. But this is beyond my instructions. I will go on with my speech in praise of you, and then get to the heart of my message.

Olivia Go right to what is important in it. I excuse you from the praise.

Viola Alas, I took a lot of trouble to learn it, and it's very poetical.

Olivia It is more likely therefore to be false. Please, do not speak it. I heard you were impudent at my gates, and permitted you to come in more to satisfy my curiosity than to hear what you had to say. If you're just mad, go away. If you're sane, be brief. There's no full moon to encourage me to take part in such a lunatic conversation.

Maria [*to* **Viola**] Will you hoist sail, sir? Here's the way out.

Viola [*to* **Maria**] No, good sailor. I'm to stay in port a while longer. [*To* **Olivia**, *referring to* **Maria**] Sweet lady, please pacify your giant.

Olivia Say what's on your mind.

Viola I am a messenger.

Olivia Surely, you have some terrifying message to deliver, if even the introduction is so fearful. State your business.

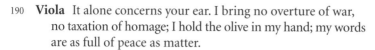

190 **Viola** It alone concerns your ear. I bring no overture of war, no taxation of homage; I hold the olive in my hand; my words are as full of peace as matter.

Olivia Yet you began rudely. What are you? What would you?

195 **Viola** The rudeness that hath appeared in me have I learned from my entertainment. What I am, and what I would, are as secret as maidenhead; to your ears, divinity; to any other's, profanation.

Olivia Give us the place alone; we will hear this divinity.

[*Exeunt* **Maria** *and* **Attendants**]

200   Now, sir; what is your text?

Viola Most sweet lady –

Olivia A comfortable doctrine, and much may be said of it. Where lies your text?

Viola In Orsino's bosom.

205 **Olivia** In his bosom! In what chapter of his bosom?

Viola To answer by the method, in the first of his heart.

Olivia O! I have read it; it is heresy. Have you no more to say?

Viola Good madam, let me see your face.

210 **Olivia** Have you any commission from your lord to negotiate with my face? You are now out of your text; but we will draw the curtain and show you the picture. (*Unveiling*) Look you, sir; such a one I was this present; is't not well done?

Viola Excellently done, if God did all.

215 **Olivia** 'Tis in grain, sir; 'twill endure wind and weather.

Viola It is only for you to hear. I bring no declaration of war, no demand for tribute payments. I hold the olive branch in my hand. My words are as peaceful as they are important.

Olivia Yet you began by being rude. Who are you? What do you want?

Viola The rudeness I showed resulted from the way I was treated when I arrived. Who I am and what I want are as secret as virginity—sacred if heard by you; profane if heard by others.

Olivia [*to* **Attendants**] Leave us. We will hear these holy words. [**Maria** *and* **Attendants** *leave*] Now, sir, what is your sacred text?

Viola Most sweet lady—

Olivia A comforting doctrine, with much to recommend it. Where does it come from?

Viola From Orsino's heart.

Olivia From his heart? From what chapter of his heart?

Viola To answer in the same way, in the first chapter of his heart.

Olivia Oh, I've read it! It's false. Have you no more to say?

Viola Good madam, let me see your face.

Olivia Have you been instructed by your lord to negotiate with my face? Now you are wandering from your sacred text. But we will draw the curtain and show you the picture. [*Lifting her veil*] Look, sir: this is a recent portrait of me. Isn't it well done?

Viola It's excellently done, if God did all of it.

Olivia The colors won't run, sir. They'll endure wind and weather.

Viola 'Tis beauty truly blent, whose red and white
Nature's own sweet and cunning hand laid on;
Lady, you are the cruell'st she alive,
If you will lead these graces to the grave
220   And leave the world no copy.

Olivia O, sir, I will not be so hard-hearted! I will give out
divers schedules of my beauty; it shall be inventoried, and
every particle and utensil labelled to my will, as, Item, Two
lips indifferent red; Item, Two grey eyes with lids to them;
225   Item, One neck, one chin, and so forth. Were you sent hither
to praise me?

Viola I see you what you are; you are too proud;
But, if you were the devil, you are fair.
My lord and master loves you; O! such love
230   Could be but recompensed, though you were crowned
The nonpareil of beauty.

Olivia   How does he love me?

Viola With adorations, fertile tears,
With groans that thunder love, with sighs of fire.

235 **Olivia** Your lord does know my mind; I cannot love him;
Yet I suppose him virtuous, know him noble,
Of great estate, of fresh and stainless youth;
In voices well divulged, free, learned, and valiant;
And in dimension and the shape of nature
240   A gracious person; but yet I cannot love him.
He might have took his answer long ago.

Viola If I did love you in my master's flame,
With such a suffering, such a deadly life,
In your denial I would find no sense;
245   I would not understand it.

Olivia   Why, what would you?

Viola Make me a willow cabin at your gate,
And call upon my soul within the house;

Viola It is beauty perfectly blended, whose red and white were painted by nature's own skillful hand. Lady, you are the cruelest woman alive, if you take all this beauty to the grave and leave the world no copy.

Olivia Oh, sir, I will not be so hard-hearted. I will publish several catalogs of my beauty. It shall be inventoried, and every article and item labeled as I see fit. For example: item, two lips, somewhat red; item, two gray eyes, with lids attached; item, one neck, one chin, and so forth. Were you sent here to "appraise" me?

Viola I see what you are. You are too proud. But even if you were the devil, you are beautiful. My lord and master loves you. Oh, such love could be only even repaid if you were crowned as the most beautiful woman in the world!

Olivia How does he love me?

Viola With adoration, with many tears, with deep groans of love, with passionate sighs.

Olivia Your lord knows my decision: I cannot love him. However, I believe him to be virtuous, know him to be noble, very wealthy, of fresh and innocent youth, well spoken of, generous, well-educated, and brave. And in his physical form a handsome person. But I cannot love him. He should have accepted his answer long ago.

Viola If I loved you as intensely as my master does, with such suffering, with such wretchedness, your refusal would seem senseless to me. I would not understand it.

Olivia Why, what would you do?

Viola I would build myself a cabin of willow branches at your gate, and cry out to my soul within your house. I would write

Write loyal cantons of contemnèd love,
250 And sing them loud even in the dead of night;
Holla your name to the reverberate hills,
And make the babbling gossip of the air
Cry out 'Olivia!' O, you should not rest
Between the elements of air and earth
255 But you should pity me!

Olivia You might do much. What is your parentage?

Viola Above my fortunes, yet my state is well:
I am a gentleman.

Olivia   Get you to your lord;
260 I cannot love him. Let him send no more,
Unless, perchance, you come to me again,
To tell me how he takes it. Fare you well;
I thank you for your pains; spend this for me.

Viola I am no fee'd post, lady; keep your purse;
265 My master, not myself, lacks recompense.
Love make his heart of flint that you shall love,
And let your fervour, like my master's, be
Placed in contempt! Farewell, fair cruelty.

                                              [*Exit*]

Olivia 'What is your parentage?'
270 'Above my fortunes, yet my state is well;
I am a gentleman.' I'll be sworn thou art;
Thy tongue, thy face, thy limbs, actions, and spirit,
Do give thee five-fold blazon. Not too fast; soft! soft! –
Unless the master were the man. Now now!
275 Even so quickly may one catch the plague?
Methinks I feel this youth's perfections,
With an invisible and subtle stealth
To creep in at mine eyes. Well, let it be.
What, ho! Malvolio!

[*Enter* **Malvolio**]

faithful songs about despised love, and sing them loudly even in the middle of the night. I would shout your name to the resounding hills, and make the echoes cry out, "Olivia!" Oh, you would find no rest between the air and earth unless you took pity on me!

Olivia You might achieve much. What is your rank?

Viola Above my present fortune. But my social standing is good. I am a gentleman.

Olivia Go back to your lord. I cannot love him. Let him send no one else to see me—unless, perhaps, you come to me again to tell me how he takes it. Farewell. I thank you for your trouble. [*She offers* **Viola** *a purse of money*] Spend this for me.

Viola I am no messenger to be tipped, lady. Keep your purse. It's my master, not me, who lacks payment. May love make the heart of the man you love as hard as flint, and let your passion, like my master's, be despised! Farewell, cruel beauty!

[**Viola** *exits*]

Olivia "What is your rank?" "Above my present fortune. But my social standing is good. I am a gentleman." I would swear you are! Your voice, your face, your form, movements, and spirit are the fivefold sign of an aristocrat. Not so fast! Stop! Wait a minute! But if the master were the man. What's this? May one catch the plague as quickly as this? I think that I feel this young man's perfections penetrating my sight with an invisible and delicate influence. Well, so be it. Come here, Malvolio!

[**Malvolio** *enters*]

280 **Malvolio**   Here, madam, at your service.

Olivia Run after that same peevish messenger,
     The county's man; he left this ring behind him,
     Would I or not; tell him I'll none of it.
     Desire him not to flatter with his lord,
285   Nor hold him up with hopes; I am not for him.
     If that the youth will come this way tomorrow,
     I'll give him reasons for 't. Hie thee, Malvolio.

Malvolio Madam, I will.

                                                    [*Exit*]

Olivia I do I know not what, and fear to find
290   Mine eye too great a flatterer for my mind.
     Fate, show thy force; ourselves we do not owe;
     What is decreed must be, and be this so.

                                                    [*Exit*]

Malvolio Here, madam, at your service.

Olivia Run after that rude messenger that was just here—the count's servant. [*She gives* **Malvolio** *a ring*] He left this ring when he left, whether I wanted it or not. Tell him I won't accept it. Request that he not encourage his lord, or hold out false hopes to him. I am not for him. If the young man will come back here tomorrow, I'll give him the reasons why. Hurry, Malvolio.

Malvolio I will, madam.

[**Malvolio** *exits*]

Olivia I don't know what I'm doing. I'm afraid that my eyes are deceiving my mind. Fate, show your power. We do not control ourselves. Whatever will be, will be. And be this so.

[**Olivia** *exits*]

Comprehension **Check What You Know**

1. Explain what Duke Orsino tells you about himself and his love for Olivia in his very first speech in the play.

2. An author can use *foreshadowing* to insert clues about events that will occur later on in a story. In Scene 2, what are examples of foreshadowing?

3. Viola disguised herself as a young man and joined the Duke's court. How does she explain her action?

4. In Scene 3, Maria and Sir Toby talk about Sir Andrew. Compare and contrast their assessments of his character. Who is more reliable?

5. In Scene 3, Sir Toby, Sir Andrew, and Maria exchange a parade of outrageous puns on sex, sword-fighting, and courting. What does this section tell you about each person's intelligence and wit?

6. Why does Duke Orsino send Viola/Cesario to Olivia's court? Why does he feel that Cesario may be his most successful spokesman?

7. Why don't Feste and Malvolio like each other? Whose side is Olivia on in the disagreement? Why does Malvolio seem out of place at Olivia's court?

8. What arguments does Viola make to try to convince Olivia to love the Duke? How does the conversation backfire?

Activities & Role-Playing **Classes or Book Clubs**

A Tumble of Emotions When we first see Viola, she is in a real fix. What challenges face her? What emotions must she be feeling, and how does she deal with those feelings? Is there a difference between the way Viola handles her situation and the way that Olivia faces hers? What would these two women say to

©Robbie Jack/CORBIS

each other about love and loss if they were to meet before Viola becomes Cesario? Working with a partner, role-play Viola and Olivia and explore these women's attitudes and perspectives.

Who's This? List the distinctive characteristics of the upstairs world and the downstairs world. Then discuss how to make the differences clear to an audience. How would you use costumes? Sets? Actors with no lines? Remember, although the downstairs world is, perhaps, more scruffy, it still is the place where carnival is celebrated most clearly. The upstairs world is more orderly, but it is still a place where the worship of love is pretty irrational.

Discussion Classes or Book Clubs

1. Early in Act I we learn about Olivia's grief over the death of her brother. But she speaks of her sorrow only during her short exchange with Feste before Viola arrives at the court. Then she almost instantly falls in love with Cesario. Discuss how timing is important in our initial impression of Olivia. If she had delivered long speeches about her sorrow and her plans for the next few years, how would your opinions of Olivia change?

2. The lyrics of an old 1940s song include these lines:

    Falling in love with love is falling for make-believe
    Falling in love with love is playing the fool
    I was unwise with eyes unable to see

    Discuss how these lines apply to Duke Orsino. Then change the words, and discuss what it means to "fall in love with grief." Is this what Olivia has done? Explain your answer.

Suggestions for Writing Improve Your Skills

1. Instead of saying that Duke Orsino is ridiculous and overwrought, most commentators say he is foolish but worthy of respect. How do you feel about the Duke? Consider both his statements and actions and those of others. Then pretend you are a new courtier in Orsino's court. Write a letter to a friend describing the Duke's character.

2. Olivia has lost her brother, so she has decided to mourn for seven years. Viola has lost her brother, as well, but her response is much different. Write a few paragraphs comparing and contrasting the two women.

3. First, Viola insists that she isn't sure which woman is Olivia. Then she asks Olivia what right she has to refuse to marry. Finally Viola speaks lyrically of the Duke's love. Why is this approach a good one?

All the World's a Stage Introduction

Illyria's carnival world is filled with fanciful declarations of love, drunken antics in the kitchen, and masquerade. Viola, disguised as Cesario, has secretly fallen in love with Orsino. Lady Olivia vowed to have nothing to do with any man for seven years but has fallen in love with Cesario. And Sir Toby and Sir Andrew sing, dance, and pun away their time.

One person is unaffected—Malvolio. By the end of Act 1, he has come into conflict with Feste, the wise fool. (Malvolio does not understand foolery.) Malvolio is asking for trouble, and he's about to get it.

What's in a Name? Characters

In Act 2 Antonio and Sebastian enter the play. Antonio is a sea captain (perhaps a pirate . . .) who rescued Viola's brother Sebastian. Since then the two have become very good friends. They'll add even more confusion to Illyria.

The list of pairs in the world of *Twelfth Night* is growing. There are Viola and Sebastian, almost identical twins. Their love was made clear in Act 1, when Viola said that since her brother was in Elysium (heaven), she should not be on Earth. Viola and the Duke are another pair (although the Duke thinks Viola is a man). Still another pair is the Duke and Olivia, although she wishes they were not. As the play continues, pairs will continue to form.

COME WHAT MAY Things to Watch For

Then there's this pair: "upstairs" and "downstairs." Upstairs is the world of the ruling class, of Viola, the Duke, and Olivia. Here, love is a matter of spirit and longing. As the Duke says, his passion is best accompanied by music and flowers. Later Viola/Cesario tells Olivia that Orsino loves her "With groans that thunder love, with sighs of fire." When you picture Orsino, do you see him on the deck of a sailing ship, defending his love from bandits? More likely, you see him lying on a couch, examining a perfect rose.

The downstairs world is the bawdy, intoxicated, physical world of Sir Toby and Sir Andrew. When Sir Andrew meets Maria, Sir Toby tells him to *accost* her. Sir Andrew mistakes it for Maria's name. Actually Toby was telling Andrew to seduce her. Sir Toby's world is one of aggressive, physical love—no roses for him.

All Our Yesterdays Historical and Social Context

In Twelfth Night celebrations, a man was chosen to be the Lord of Misrule, the night's madcap ruler. In *Twelfth Night,* the Lord of Misrule is probably Sir Toby Belch, so Elizabethan audiences would allow him a great deal of leeway. They'd understand as he pounds on the piano and dances in the middle of the night. They also wouldn't be offended when he takes advantage of Sir Andrew—that only shows Toby's wit and cleverness.

During the Renaissance, class boundaries were loosening, so a servant could rise from, say, a footman to a page or even to a steward. Both servants and masters had responsibilities and duties in their relationships with each other. A master was to house, feed, and dress his servants well. Servants were to be dignified, respectful, and attentive. Also, four times a year they were paid, and they could also receive tips. In *Twelfth Night,* Feste gets tips for his songs and "fooling."

This world is not a democracy. Social class is important—in Act 1 Viola/Cesario made it clear that she/he is a "gentleman." In the action to come, class will be an important issue.

The Play's the Thing Staging

Shakespeare wrote his plays for a company of players—a group of actors who worked together all the time—so he knew their skills and abilities. When Shakespeare wrote *Twelfth Night,* he designed the role of Feste for Robert Armin. To take advantage of Armin's intelligence and talent, Shakespeare made Feste a literate, clever, and sarcastic commentator. Armin also was an accomplished singer, so Shakespeare included several songs.

Many actors played instruments—like a minstrel, Feste probably accompanied himself on the lute. Some songs were written specifically for a play, but others were familiar folk songs, street cries, and love ballads. Today's advertising campaigns that feature pop music are using the same technique.

My Words Fly Up Language

Extravagant wordplay continues in Scene 2, when Feste joins Sir Toby and Sir Andrew and talks about a picture of "we three," a popular joke of the times. The picture shows only two asses. The third is the person looking at the picture. Nonsense sentences and made-up words also are crucial to the wordplay.

In Act 2 Maria says Malvolio is a *puritan.* Sir Andrew thinks she's referring to the Puritan religious group, but she says she is only describing Malvolio's character. Malvolio dislikes jovial events, fooling around—anything that lacks high seriousness. Olivia said the same thing in Act 1, although she wasn't as angry as Maria. Because Malvolio's character blocks the spirit of Twelfth Night, he will receive very little sympathy from the audience.

The Duke and Cesario compare the way men and women experience love. Again you'll hear about the humours and the organs of the body that control emotions. For instance, the Duke will claim that in women love doesn't originate in the liver. He's saying that women do not feel love as deeply as men.

Act II

Scene I

The Sea-coast. Enter **Antonio** *and* **Sebastian**

Antonio Will you stay no longer, nor will you not that I go with you?

Sebastian By your patience, no. My stars shine darkly over me; the malignancy of my fate might, perhaps, distemper
5 yours; therefore I shall crave of you your leave that I may bear my evils alone. It were a bad recompense for your love, to lay any of them on you.

Antonio Let me yet know of you whither you are bound.

Sebastian No, sooth, sir; my determinate voyage is mere
10 extravagancy. But I perceive in you so excellent a touch of modesty, that you will not extort from me what I am willing to keep in; therefore it charges me in manners the rather to express myself. You must know of me then, Antonio, my name is Sebastian, which I called Roderigo. My father was
15 that Sebastian of Messaline, whom I know you have heard of. He left behind him myself and a sister, both born in an hour; if the heavens had been pleased, would we had so ended! But you, sir, altered that; for some hour before you took me from the breach of the sea was my sister drowned.

20 **Antonio** Alas the day!

Sebastian A lady, sir, though it was said she much resembled me, was yet of many accounted beautiful; but, though I could

The seacoast of Illyria. Viola's brother **Sebastian** *enters with* **Antonio,** *a sea captain.*

Antonio Won't you stay any longer? Do you not wish that I go with you?

Sebastian Pardon me, but no. My future looks dark. My evil fate might possibly affect your fortunes. Therefore, I shall beg your permission to bear my evils alone. To burden you with any of them would be a bad way to repay you for your love.

Antonio Let me know which way you're going.

Sebastian No, truly, sir. My travel plan is merely aimless wandering. But I see that you are so polite that you will not force from me what I wish to keep secret. Therefore, it would be courteous for me to tell you instead. You must know then, Antonio, that my name is Sebastian, though I called myself Rodrigo. My father was that Sebastian of Messaline that I'm sure you've heard of. He left behind him myself and a sister, both born in the same hour. God willing, I wish we had died the same way! But you, sir, changed that, for about an hour before you pulled me from the surf, my sister was drowned.

Antonio What a sad day!

Sebastian Although it was said she resembled me very much, sir, she was a lady that many people considered beautiful. But though I could not go to that length in my admiration, yet

not with such estimable wonder overfar believe that, yet
thus far I will boldly publish her; she bore a mind that Envy
25 could not but call fair. She is drowned already, sir, with salt
water, though I seem to drown her remembrance again with
more.

Antonio Pardon me, sir, your bad entertainment.

Sebastian O good Antonio! forgive me your trouble.

30 **Antonio** If you will not murder me for my love, let me be
your servant.

Sebastian If you will not undo what you have done, that is,
kill him whom you have recovered, desire it not. Fare ye
well at once; my bosom is full of kindness; and I am yet so
35 near the manners of my mother that upon the least occasion
more mine eyes will tell tales of me. I am bound to the
Count Orsino's court; farewell.

[*Exit*]

Antonio The gentleness of all the gods go with thee!
I have many enemies in Orsino's court,
40 Else would I very shortly see thee there;
But, come what may, I do adore thee so,
That danger shall seem sport, and I will go.

[*Exit*]

I will go this far in my praise of her: she had a mind that even her enemies would have to call fine. [*He begins to weep*] She is drowned already, sir, in salt water; and now I am beginning to drown her memory again with more.

Antonio Pardon me, sir, for my humble hospitality.

Sebastian Oh good Antonio, forgive me for all the trouble I've put you to.

Antonio If you don't want me to die from love of you, let me be your servant.

Sebastian If you don't want to undo what you have done, that is, kill the one you rescued, don't ask it. Let me say farewell right now. My heart is full of tenderness, and I am still such a child that with just a little more prompting my tears will embarrass me. I am going to the Count Orsino's court. Farewell.

[**Sebastian** *exits*]

Antonio The gentleness of all the gods go with you! I have many enemies at Orsino's court; otherwise I would see you there very soon. But whatever might happen, I love you so much that danger shall seem pleasant. So I'll go.

[**Antonio** *exits*]

Act II

Scene II

A Street. Enter **Viola;** *Malvolio following.*

Malvolio Were you not even now with the Countess Olivia?

Viola Even now, sir; on a moderate pace I have since arrived
but hither.

Malvolio She returns this ring to you, sir; you might have
5   saved me my pains, to have taken it away yourself. She adds,
moreover, that you should put your lord into a desperate
assurance she will none of him. And one thing more: that
you be never so hardy to come again in his affairs, unless it
be to report your lord's taking of this. Receive it so.

10 **Viola** She took the ring of me; I'll none of it.

Malvolio Come, sir, you peevishly threw it to her; and her
will is it should be so returned; if it be worth stooping for,
there it lies in your eye; if not, be it his that finds it.

[Exit]

Viola I left no ring with her; what means this lady?
15 Fortune forbid my outside have not charmed her!
She made good view of me; indeed so much
That sure methought her eyes had lost her tongue,
For she did speak in starts distractedly.
She loves me, sure; the cunning of her passion
20 Invites me in this churlish messenger.

A street near Olivia's house. **Viola** *enters, followed by* **Malvolio**.

Malvolio Weren't you with the Countess Olivia just now?

Viola Just now, sir. Walking steadily, I have only got this far.

Malvolio She is returning this ring to you, sir. You might have spared me my trouble, by taking it away yourself. She adds, in addition, that you should make it completely clear to your lord that she will have nothing to do with him. And one thing more: that you should not be so bold as to come again on his behalf, unless it would be to report how your lord has taken it back. Take it now.

Viola She took the ring from me. I won't take it back.

Malvolio Come, sir, you rudely threw it to her, and her desire is that it should be returned in the same way. [*He throws it down*] If it is worth stooping for, there it is. Otherwise, let it be his that finds it.

[**Malvolio** *exits*]

Viola [*picking up the ring*] I left no ring with her. What does this lady mean? Heaven forbid that she was charmed by my looks! She examined me closely; indeed, so closely that using her eyes seemed to cause her to be tongue-tied, because she spoke in a halting, disturbed manner. It's certain—she loves me! Cunning in her passion, she uses this rude messenger to invite me back.

None of my lord's ring! Why, he sent her none.
I am the man; if it be so, as 'tis,
Poor lady, she were better love a dream.
Disguise, I see thou art a wickedness
25   Wherein the pregnant enemy does much.
How easy is it for the proper-false
In women's waxen hearts to set their forms!
Alas! our frailty is the cause, not we,
For such as we are made of, such we be.

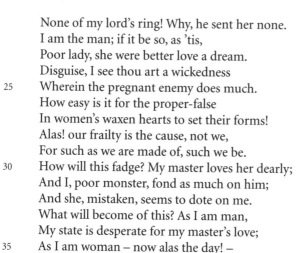

30   How will this fadge? My master loves her dearly;
And I, poor monster, fond as much on him;
And she, mistaken, seems to dote on me.
What will become of this? As I am man,
My state is desperate for my master's love;
35   As I am woman – now alas the day! –
What thriftless sighs shall poor Olivia breathe!
O time, thou must untangle this, not I;
It is too hard a knot for me to untie.

(
Ryhming
couplet / Metaphor.

[*Exit*]

She won't accept my lord's ring? Why, he sent her none. I'm her man. If this is true—and it is—poor lady, she might as well love a dream. Disguise, I see that you are a wickedness that gives great opportunity to the cunning devil. How easy it is for false but handsome men to make an impression on women's soft hearts! Alas, our weakness is the cause, not ourselves; for we must be what we are made of. How will this turn out? My master loves her dearly. And I, poor creature, am just as fond of him. And she, mistakenly, seems to dote on me. What will become of this? As a man, I have no hope of winning my master's love. As I am a woman—which I now must regret—what hopeless sighs shall poor Olivia breathe. Oh, time, you must untangle this; I can't. It's too hard a knot for me to untie.

[**Viola** *exits*]

Act II

Scene III

Olivia's House. Enter **Sir Toby Belch** *and* **Sir Andrew Aguecheek.**

Sir Toby Approach, Sir Andrew: now to be a-bed after midnight is to be up betimes; and *diluculo surgere,* thou knowest –

Sir Andrew Nay, by my troth, I know not; but I know, to be
5 up late is to be up late.

Sir Toby A false conclusion; I hate it as an unfilled can. To be up after midnight, and to go to bed then, is early; so that to go to bed after midnight is to go to bed betimes. Does not our life consist of the four elements?

10 **Sir Andrew** Faith, so they say; but I think it rather consists of eating and drinking.

Sir Toby Thou'rt a scholar; let us therefore eat and drink. Marian, I say! a stoup of wine!

[*Enter* **Feste**]

Sir Andrew Here comes the fool, i' faith.

15 **Feste** How now, my hearts! Did you never see the picture of 'we three'?

Sir Toby Welcome, ass. Now let's have a catch.

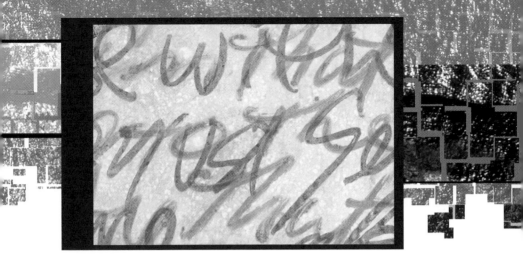

A room in Olivia's house. **Sir Toby Belch** *and* **Sir Andrew Aguecheek** *enter.*

Sir Toby Come on, Sir Andrew. Not to be in bed after midnight is to be up early. And you remember the Latin proverb, "Early to rise . . . "—

Sir Andrew No, indeed, I don't. But I know that to be up late is to be up late.

Sir Toby A false conclusion. I hate it as much as an empty tankard. If you're up after midnight, and go to bed then, it's early in the morning. So that to go to bed after midnight is to go to bed early. Doesn't our life consist of the four elements of earth, air, water, and fire?

Sir Andrew Indeed, so they say. But I think it really consists of eating and drinking.

Sir Toby You are a scholar. Let us therefore eat and drink. [*Calling to* **Maria**] Maria, I say! a jug of wine!

[**Feste** *enters*]

Sir Andrew Here comes the fool, indeed.

Feste Greetings, friends! [*He puts his arms around both of them*] Didn't you ever see the picture of "we three"? [*Referring to a picture of two fools or asses; the third is the viewer*]

Sir Toby Welcome, ass. Now let's have a catch. [*Referring to a round song for three or more voices in which words overlap for humorous effect*]

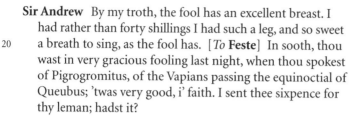

Sir Andrew By my troth, the fool has an excellent breast. I
had rather than forty shillings I had such a leg, and so sweet
20   a breath to sing, as the fool has. [*To* **Feste**] In sooth, thou
wast in very gracious fooling last night, when thou spokest
of Pigrogromitus, of the Vapians passing the equinoctial of
Queubus; 'twas very good, i' faith. I sent thee sixpence for
thy leman; hadst it?

25   **Feste** I did impeticos thy gratillity, for Malvolio's nose is no
whipstock; my lady has a white hand, and the Myrmidons are
no bottle-ale houses.

Sir Andrew Excellent! Why, this is the best fooling, when all
is done. Now, a song.

30   **Sir Toby** Come on; there is sixpence for you; let's have a song.

Sir Andrew There's a testril of me too; if one knight give a –

Feste Would you have a love-song, or a song of good life?

Sir Toby A love-song, a love-song.

Sir Andrew Ay, ay; I care not for good life.

35   **Feste** [*Singing*] *O mistress mine! where are you roaming?*
O stay and hear! your true love's coming,
That can sing both high and low.
Trip no further, pretty sweeting;
Journeys end in lovers meeting,
40   *Every wise man's son doth know.*

Sir Andrew Excellent good, i' faith.

Sir Toby Good, good.

Sir Andrew Indeed, the fool has an excellent voice. I would give forty shillings to have such a good figure and fine singing voice as the fool has. [*To* **Feste**] Truly, you were very funny last night when you spoke of Pigrogromitus and of the Vapians passing the equinoctial of Queubus. [*Referring to Feste's learned double-talk*] It was very good, indeed. I sent you sixpence for your sweetheart. Did you get it?

Feste [*using invented "high-tone" phrases*] I impetticoated your gratillity, for Malvolio sticks his nose in everything, my lady is overly refined, and beer isn't cheap at The Myrmidons tavern.

Sir Andrew Excellent! Why, this is the best kind of fooling, when all is said and done. Now, let's have a song.

Sir Toby [*giving* **Feste** *money*] Come on, there is sixpence for you. Let's have a song.

Sir Andrew [*giving* **Feste** *money*] There's sixpence from me too. If one knight gives a—

Feste Would you like a love song or a song about how good life is?

Sir Toby A love song, a love song.

Sir Andrew Yes, yes. I don't care for the good life.

Feste [*sings*]
> Oh, mistress mine! Where are you roaming?
> Oh, stay and hear! Your true love's coming,
> Who can sing both high and low.
> Trip no further, pretty sweeting,
> Journeys end in lovers' meeting,
> Every wise man's son does know.

Sir Andrew Very good, indeed!

Sir Toby Good, good.

Feste [*Singing*] *What is love? 'Tis not hereafter;*
Present mirth hath present laughter;
45   *What's to come is still unsure.*
In delay there lies no plenty;
Then come kiss me, sweet-and-twenty,
Youth's a stuff will not endure.

Sir Andrew A mellifluous voice, as I am true knight.

50 **Sir Toby** A contagious breath.

Sir Andrew Very sweet and contagious, i' faith.

Sir Toby To hear by the nose, it is dulcet in contagion. But
shall we make the welkin dance indeed? Shall we rouse the
night-owl in a catch that will draw three souls out of one
55   weaver? Shall we do that?

Sir Andrew An you love me, let's do 't; I am dog at a catch.

Feste By'r lady, sir, and some dogs will catch well.

Sir Andrew Most certain. Let our catch be, 'Thou knave'.

Feste 'Hold thy peace, thou knave', knight? I shall be
60   constrained in't to call thee knave, knight.

Sir Andrew 'Tis not the first time I have constrained one to
call me knave. Begin, fool; it begins 'Hold thy peace'.

Feste I shall never begin if I hold my peace.

Sir Andrew Good i' faith. Come, begin.

[*They sing a catch*]

[*Enter* **Maria**]

65 **Maria** What a caterwauling do you keep here! If my lady
have not called up her steward Malvolio and bid him turn
you out of doors, never trust me.

Feste [*sings*]
> What is love? It's not in the world to come;
> Present joy hath present laughter;
> What's to come is still unsure.
> In delay there lies no plenty;
> Then come kiss me, sweet and twenty,
> Youth's a stuff will not endure.

Sir Andrew A honey-sweet voice, as I am a true knight.

Sir Toby A very catching voice.

Sir Andrew Very sweet and catching, indeed.

Sir Toby If we heard with our noses, it would be sweet and catching. But shall we make the heavens dance indeed? Shall we wake the night owl by singing a catch that will draw three souls out of one weaver? Shall we do that?

Sir Andrew If you love me, let's do it. I'm a dog at a catch.

Feste Indeed, sir, and some dogs do catch well.

Sir Andrew That's certain. Let our catch be "You knave."

Feste "Hold your peace, you knave," knight? I shall be forced to call you a knave in it, knight.

Sir Andrew It won't be the first time I've forced someone to call me a knave. You start, fool. It begins, "Hold your peace."

Feste I shall never begin if I hold my peace.

Sir Andrew That's a good one. Come, begin. [*They sing the catch in turn, making a great deal of noise*]

[**Maria** *enters*]

Maria What a racket you're making! If my lady hasn't called her steward Malvolio and ordered him to throw you out, never trust me again.

Sir Toby My lady's a Cataian; we are politicians; Malvolio's a
Peg-a-Ramsey, and 'Three merry men be we'. Am not I
70 consanguineous? Am I not of her blood? Tillyvally; lady!
[*Singing*] There dwelt a man in Babylon, lady, lady! –

Feste Beshrew me, the knight's in admirable fooling.

Sir Andrew Ay, he does well enough if he be disposed, and
so do I too; he does it with a better grace, but I do it more
75 natural.

Sir Toby [*Singing*] O the twelfth day of December –

Maria For the love o' God, peace!

[*Enter* **Malvolio**]

Malvolio My masters, are you mad, or what are you? Have
you no wit, manners, nor honesty, but to gabble like tinkers
80 at this time of night? Do ye make an alehouse of my lady's
house, that ye squeak out your coziers' catches without any
mitigation or remorse of voice? Is there no respect of place,
persons, nor time in you?

Sir Toby We did keep time, sir, in our catches. Sneck up!

85 **Malvolio** Sir Toby, I must be round with you. My lady bade
me tell you that, though she harbours you as her kinsman,
she's nothing allied to your disorders. If you can separate
yourself and your misdemeanours, you are welcome to the
house; if not, an it would please you to take leave of her, she
90 is very willing to bid you farewell.

Sir Toby [*Singing*] Farewell, dear heart, since I must needs be
gone.

Maria Nay, good Sir Toby.

Feste [*Singing*] His eyes do show his days are almost done.

95 **Malvolio** Is't even so?

Sir Toby My lady's unpredictable, we are cunning, Malvolio's a fool, and [*he sings*] "Three merry men be we." Am I not a relative? Am I not of her blood? Tush! Lady! [*He sings*] "There dwelt a man in Babylon, lady, lady."

Feste Devil take me, the knight's very funny.

Sir Andrew Yes, he does well enough when he feels like it, and so do I too. He does it with more style, but I am the more natural fool.

Sir Toby [*sings*] "Oh the twelfth day of December"—

Maria For the love of God, peace!

[**Malvolio** *enters*]

Malvolio My masters, are you mad? What are you doing? Do you have no common sense, manners, or decency, but to gabble like gypsies at this time of night? Are you making my lady's house into an alehouse by squawking your shoemakers' songs as loud as you can? Do you have no respect for where you are, or other people, or what time it is?

Sir Toby We did keep time, sir, in our catches. Go hang yourself!

Malvolio Sir Toby, I must be plain-spoken with you. My lady ordered me to tell you that although she gives you a home here because you are her kinsman, she is no kin at all to your disorders. If you can keep yourself from this misconduct, you are welcome to stay on in the house. If you're not, and you would rather leave her, she is very willing to bid you farewell.

Sir Toby [*beginning to sing a ballad*] "Farewell, dear heart, since I must needs be gone."

Maria No, good Sir Toby.

Feste [*sings*] "His eyes do show his days are almost done."

Malvolio So that's how it will be?

Sir Toby [*Singing*] But I will never die.

Feste [*Singing*] Sir Toby, there you lie.

Malvolio This is much credit to you.

Sir Toby [*Singing*] Shall I bid him go?

100 **Feste** [*Singing*] What an if you do?

Sir Toby [*Singing*] Shall I bid him go, and spare not?

Feste [*Singing*] O! no, no, no, no, you dare not.

Sir Toby Out o' tune, sir! ye lie. Art any more than a
    steward? Dost thou think, because thou art virtuous, there
105   shall be no more cakes and ale?

Feste Yes, by Saint Anne; and ginger shall be hot i' the mouth
    too.

Sir Toby Thou'rt i' the right. Go, sir, rub your chain with
    crumbs. A stoup of wine, Maria!

110 **Malvolio** Mistress Mary, if you prized my lady's favour at
    anything more than contempt, you would not give means
    for this uncivil rule, she shall know of it, by this hand.

[*Exit*]

Maria Go shake your ears.

Sir Andrew 'Twere as good a deed as to drink when a man's
115   a-hungry, to challenge him the field, and then to break
    promise with him and make a fool of him.

Sir Toby Do't, knight; I'll write thee a challenge; or I'll
    deliver thy indignation to him by word of mouth.

Maria Sweet Sir Toby, be patient for tonight; since the youth
120   of the count's was today with my lady, she is much out of

Sir Toby [*sings*] "But I will never die."

Feste [*improvising*] "Sir Toby, there you lie."

Malvolio This behavior does great credit to you.

Sir Toby [*sings*] "Shall I tell him to go?"

Feste [*sings*] "And what if you do?"

Sir Toby [*sings*] "Shall I tell him to go, and care not?"

Feste [*sings*] "Oh, no, no, no, no, you dare not!"

Sir Toby [*to* **Feste**] That's out of tune, sir! You lie. [*To* **Malvolio**] Are you anything more than a steward? Do you think, because you are virtuous, there will be no more cakes and ale, no more merrymaking?

Feste Yes, by Saint Anne, and ginger will still taste hot too!

Sir Toby [*to* **Feste**] You're right. [*To* **Malvolio**] Go, sir, polish up your steward's chain. A jug of wine, Maria!

Malvolio Mistress Mary, if you valued my lady's good opinion at anything higher than contempt, you would not provide the drink that aids this rude behavior. She shall hear of this, by this hand.

[**Malvolio** *exits*]

Maria Go and shake your donkey's ears!

Sir Andrew It would feel as good as to drink when you're hungry to challenge him to duel, then not show up, and make a fool of him.

Sir Toby Do it, knight. I'll write a challenge for you or I'll deliver your insult to him by word of mouth.

Maria Sweet Sir Toby, be patient for tonight. Since the Duke's young man visited my lady today, she has been very quiet. For Monsieur Malvolio, let me alone with him; if I do not gull him into a nayword, and make him a common recreation, do not think I have wit enough to lie straight in my bed. I know I can do it.

125 **Sir Toby** Possess us, possess us.

Sir Andrew Tell us something of him.

Maria Marry, sir, sometimes he is a kind of Puritan.

Sir Andrew O! if I thought that, I'd beat him like a dog.

Sir Toby What, for being a Puritan? Thy exquisite reason, 130   dear knight!

Sir Andrew I have no exquisite reason for 't, but I have reason good enough.

Maria The devil a Puritan that he is, or anything constantly, but a time-pleaser, an affectioned ass, that cons state without 135   book, and utters it by great swarths; the best persuaded of himself; so crammed, as he thinks, with excellences, that it is his ground of faith that all that look on him love him; and on that vice in him will my revenge find notable cause to work.

140 **Sir Toby** What wilt thou do?

Maria I will drop in his way some obscure epistles of love; wherein, by the colour of his beard, the shape of his leg, the manner of his gait, the expressure of his eye, forehead, and complexion, he shall find himself most feelingly personated. 145   I can write very like my lady your niece; on a forgotten matter we can hardly make distinction of our hands.

Sir Toby Excellent! I smell a device.

Sir Andrew I have 't in my nose, too.

Sir Toby He shall think, by the letters that thou wilt drop, 150   that they come from my niece, and that she's in love with him.

nervous. As for Monsieur Malvolio, leave him to me. If I do not trick him so that he becomes a byword for stupidity and make him a general laughingstock, don't believe I have brains enough to lie straight in my bed. I know I can do it.

Sir Toby Tell us, tell us something of it.

Sir Andrew Yes, tell us something about him.

Maria Indeed, sir, sometimes he is a kind of puritan.

Sir Andrew Oh, if I thought that, I'd beat him like a dog!

Sir Toby What, for being a puritan? What's your clever reason for that, dear knight?

Sir Andrew I have no clever reason for it, but I have good enough reason.

Maria He's no real puritan or anything consistently. He's a conformist, an affected ass that is always imitating the speech and manners of his betters. He has the highest opinion of himself. He is so crammed with excellences—in his own view—that it is his firm belief that all who see him love him. And it is on that weakness of his that my revenge will work itself out very effectively.

Sir Toby What will you do?

Maria I will drop in his path some ambiguous love letters. In them he will find himself exactly described by the color of his beard, the shape of his leg, the manner of his walk, and the look of his eye, forehead, and face. I can write very like my lady, your niece. On a note we've both forgotten, we can hardly decide whose handwriting it is.

Sir Toby Excellent! I smell a scheme.

Sir Andrew I can smell it too.

Sir Toby He shall think by the letters that you drop that they come from my niece, and that she is in love with him.

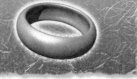

Maria My purpose is, indeed, a horse of that colour.

Sir Andrew And your horse now would make him an ass.

Maria Ass, I doubt not.

155 **Sir Andrew** O! 'twill be admirable.

Maria Sport royal, I warrant you; I know my physic will work
with him. I will plant you two, and let the fool make a third,
where he shall find the letter; observe his construction of it.
For this night, to bed, and dream on the event. Farewell.

[*Exit*]

160 **Sir Toby** Good night, Penthesilea.

Sir Andrew Before me, she's a good wench.

Sir Toby She's a beagle, true-bred, and one that adores me;
what o' that?

Sir Andrew I was adored once too.

165 **Sir Toby** Let's to bed, knight. Thou hadst need send for
more money.

Sir Andrew If I cannot recover your niece, I am a foul way
out.

Sir Toby Send for money, knight; if thou hast her not i' the
170 end, call me cut.

Sir Andrew If I do not, never trust me, take it how you will.

Sir Toby Come, come, I'll go burn some sack; 'tis too late to
go to bed now. Come, knight; come knight.

[*Exeunt*]

Maria My plan is indeed a horse of that color.

Sir Andrew And your horse will make an ass of him.

Maria Ass I have no doubt.

Sir Andrew That will be admirable!

Maria Great sport, I guarantee it. I know my medicine will work with him. I will hide you two, along with Fabian, where Malvolio will find the letter. Watch how he interprets it. For this night, to bed, and dream of what's to happen. Farewell.

[**Maria** *exits*]

Sir Toby [*to the tiny* **Maria**] Good night, my Amazon Queen.

Sir Andrew By my soul, she's a good lass!

Sir Toby [*again referring to* **Maria***'s small size*] She's a beagle, true-bred. And she adores me. What do you think of that?

Sir Andrew I was adored once too.

Sir Toby Let's go to bed, knight. You need to send for some more money.

Sir Andrew If I can't win your niece, I'm going to be a lot poorer.

Sir Toby Send for more money, knight. If you don't get her in the end, call me a horse's tail.

Sir Andrew If I don't, never trust me. You can take it any way you like.

Sir Toby Come, come. I'll go warm up some wine. It's too late to go to bed now. Come, knight. Come, knight.

[*They exit*]

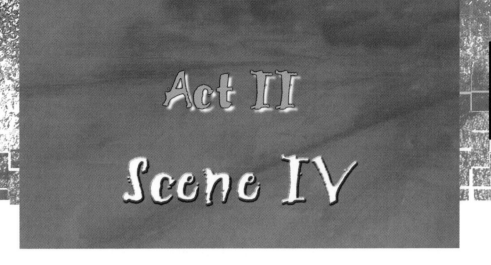

Act II

Scene IV

The Duke's Palace. Enter **Duke, Viola, Curio,** *and others.*

Duke Give me some music. Now, good morrow, friends.
Now, good Cesario, but that piece of song,
That old and antique song we heard last night;
Methought it did relieve my passion much,
5 More than light airs and recollected terms
Of these most brisk and giddy-paced times.
Come; but one verse.

Curio He is not here, so please your lordship, that should
sing it.

10 **Duke** Who was it?

Curio Feste, the jester, my lord; a fool that the lady Olivia's
father took much delight in. He is about the house.

Duke Seek him out, and play the tune the while.

[*Exit* **Curio**]

Come hither, boy: if ever thou shalt love,
15 In the sweet pangs of it remember me;
For such as I am all true lovers are,
Unstaid and skittish in all motions else
Save in the constant image of the creature
That is beloved. How dost thou like this tune?

A room in Duke Orsino's palace. The **Duke, Viola, Curio,** *and others enter.*

Duke Play me some music. Now, friends; good morning. Good Cesario, just let us now hear that old and antique song we heard last night. I thought that it greatly eased my passion, much more than the trivial melodies and artificial words of these brisk and giddy-paced times. Come, just one verse.

Curio The one who should sing it isn't here, so please your lordship.

Duke Who is that?

Curio Feste the jester, my lord, a fool that greatly delighted the Lady Olivia's father. He is around the house.

Duke Go find him, and play the tune meanwhile. [**Curio** *exits and music plays*]

[*To* **Viola**] Come here, boy. If ever you are in love, remember me in the sweet pain of it. Because the way I am, all true lovers are: giddy and fickle in all thoughts and feelings except their obsession with the one who is beloved. How do you like this tune?

Dramatic
_ Irony

99

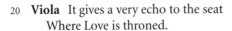

20 **Viola** It gives a very echo to the seat
   Where Love is throned.

   Duke   Thou dost speak masterly.
   My life upon 't, young though thou art, thine eye
   Hath stayed upon some favour that it loves;
25 Hath it not, boy?

   Viola   A little, by your favour.

   Duke What kind of woman is't?

   Viola   Of your complexion.

   Duke She is not worth thee, then. What years, i'faith?

30 **Viola** About your years, my lord.

   Duke Too old, by heaven. Let still the woman take
   An elder than herself, so wears she to him,
   So sways she level in her husband's heart;
   For, boy, however we do praise ourselves,
35 Our fancies are more giddy and unfirm,
   More longing, wavering, sooner lost and worn,
   Than women's are.

   Viola   I think it well, my lord.

   Duke Then let thy love be younger than thyself,
40 Or thy affection cannot hold the bent;
   For women are as roses, whose fair flower
   Being once displayed, doth fall that very hour.

   Viola And so they are; alas, that they are so!
   To die, even when they to perfection grow.

   [*Enter* **Curio** *and* **Feste**]

45 **Duke** O, fellow! come, the song we had last night.
   Mark it, Cesario; it is old and plain;
   The spinsters and the knitters in the sun,
   And the free maids that weave their thread with bones,

Viola It truly echoes what the heart feels.

Duke You speak like one who has known love. Upon my life, young as you are, your eye has lingered on some face that it loves. Hasn't it, boy?

Viola A little, if you please.

Duke What kind of woman is she?

Viola Of your complexion.

Duke She isn't good enough for you, then. How old, indeed?

Viola About your age, my lord.

Duke Too old, by heaven. Always let the woman take a man older than herself. In that way, she adapts herself to him. So she finds a firm place in her husband's heart. For, boy, however much we men praise ourselves, our affections are more giddy and fickle, more yearning, unsteady, sooner lost and worn out, than women's are.

Viola I'm sure that's true, my lord.

Duke Then, make sure your loved one is younger than you are, or your affection won't last. For women are like roses, whose beautiful flowers, as soon as they bloom, begin to fade at once.

Viola Yes, they are like that. Alas, that they are! To die, just when they have reached perfection!

[**Curio** and **Feste** enter]

Duke Oh, fellow! Come, let's hear the song we had last night. Note it, Cesario. It's old and plain. The spinning-women and the knitters in the sunshine, and the carefree maidens that

Do use to chant it; it is silly sooth,
50 And dallies with the innocence of love,
Like the old age.

Feste Are you ready, sir?

Duke Ay; prithee sing.

Feste [*Singing*] *Come away, come away, death,*
55 *And in sad cypress let me be laid;*
Fly away, fly away, breath;
I am slain by a fair cruel maid.
My shroud of white, stuck all with yew,
O! prepare it;
60 *My part of death, no one so true*
Did share it.
Not a flower, not a flower sweet,
On my black coffin let there be strown;
Not a friend, not a friend greet
65 *My poor corpse, where my bones shall be*
thrown;
A thousand thousand sighs to save,
Lay me O! where
Sad true lover never find my grave,
70 *To weep there.*

Duke There's for thy pains.

Feste No pains, sir; I take pleasure in singing, sir.

Duke I'll pay thy pleasure, then.

Feste Truly, sir, and pleasure will be paid, one time or
75 another.

Duke Give me now leave to leave thee.

Feste Now, the melancholy god protect thee, and the tailor
make thy doublet of changeable taffeta, for thy mind is a
very opal! I would have men of such constancy put to sea,
80 that their business might be everything and their intent

weave their thread, often sing it. It is simple truth, and dwells
sweetly on the innocence of love, as in the good old days.

Feste Are you ready, sir?

Duke Yes, please sing. [*Music plays*]

Feste [*sings*]
> Come away, come away, death,
>> And in sad cypress let me be laid;
> Fly away, fly away, breath;
>> I'm slain by a fair cruel maid.
> My shroud of white, stuck all with yew,
>> O! prepare it;
> My part of death, no one so true
>> Did share it.
> Not a flower, not a flower sweet,
>> On my black coffin let there be strewn;
> Not a friend, not a friend greet
>> My poor corpse, where my bones shall be thrown;
> A thousand thousand sighs to save,
>> Lay me O! where
> Sad true lover never finds my grave,
>> To weep there.

Duke [*giving* **Feste** *money*] This is for your trouble.

Feste No trouble, sir, I take pleasure in singing, sir.

Duke I'll pay for your pleasure then.

Feste Truly, sir, pleasure must be paid for, sooner or later.

Duke You may leave now.

Feste May the god of melancholy protect you, and the tailor
make your jacket of changeable taffeta, for your mind changes
like an opal changes color. I would have such changeable men
go to sea. Then their business could be everything and their

everywhere; for that's it that always makes a good voyage of nothing. Farewell.

[*Exit*]

Duke Let all the rest give place.

[*Exeunt* **Curio** *and* **Attendants**]

Once more, Cesario,

85 Get thee to yond same sovereign cruelty;
Tell her, my love, more noble than the world,
Prizes not quantity of dirty lands;
The parts that fortune hath bestowed upon her,
Tell her, I hold as giddily as fortune;
90 But 'tis that miracle and queen of gems
That nature pranks her in, attracts my soul.

Viola But if she cannot love you, sir?

Duke I cannot be so answered.

Viola   Sooth, but you must.
95 Say that some lady, as perhaps there is,
Hath for your love as great a pang of heart
As you have for Olivia; you cannot love her;
You tell her so; must she not then be answered?

Duke There is no woman's sides
100 Can bide the beating of so strong a passion
As love doth give my heart; no woman's heart
So big, to hold so much; they lack retention.
Alas! their love may be called appetite,
No motion of the liver, but the palate,
105 That suffer surfeit, cloyment, and revolt;
But mine is all as hungry as the sea,
And can digest as much. Make no compare
Between that love a woman can bear me
And that I owe Olivia.

destination anywhere. And such changeableness always makes a good voyage out of nothing. Farewell.

[**Feste** *exits*]

Duke All the rest of you may leave.

[**Curio** *and* **Attendants** *exit*]

[*To* **Viola**] Once more, Cesario, go to that same supremely cruel woman. Tell her that my love, nobler than the world, puts no value on large quantities of dirty lands. Tell her that I care for the riches that fortune has given her as little as fortune does. It is the wonderful and jewel-like beauty with which nature has adorned her that attracts my soul.

Viola But if she still cannot love you, sir?

Duke I cannot accept that answer.

Viola Truly, but you must. Suppose there were some lady—as perhaps there is—that had as painful a love for you as you do for Olivia. You cannot love her; you tell her so. Must she not accept your answer then?

Duke There is no woman's heart that could endure the beating of so great a passion as love gives to mine. No woman's heart is big enough to hold that much; they lack the grasp. Alas, their love might be called appetite—a function of taste, not passion. Their love experiences excess, weariness, and revulsion. But mine is always as hungry as the sea, and can consume as much. Make no comparison between the love a woman could have for me and that I have for Olivia.

110 **Viola**   Ay, but I know –

Duke What dost thou know?

Viola Too well what love women to men may owe;
　　In faith, they are as true of heart as we.
　　My father had a daughter loved a man,
115　As it might be, perhaps, were I a woman,
　　I should your lordship.

Duke   And what's her history?

Viola A blank, my lord. She never told her love,
　　But let concealment, like a worm i' the bud,
120　Feed on her damask cheek; she pined in thought,
　　And with a green and yellow melancholy,
　　She sat like Patience on a monument,
　　Smiling at grief. Was not this love indeed?
　　We men may say more, swear more; but indeed
125　Our shows are more than will, for still we prove
　　Much in our vows, but little in our love.

Duke But died thy sister of her love, my boy?

Viola I am all the daughters of my father's house,
　　And all the brothers too; and yet I know not.
130　Sir, shall I to this lady?

Duke   Ay, that's the theme.
　　To her in haste; give her this jewel; say
　　My love can give no place, bide no denay.

[*Exeunt*]

Viola Yes, but I know—

Duke What do you know?

Viola Too well what love women may have for men. Indeed, they are as faithful as we are. My father had a daughter who loved a man; just as, perhaps, if I were a woman, I might love your lordship.

Duke And what's her story?

Viola A blank page, my lord. She never revealed her love, but let concealment feed on her pink cheek, like a worm in a flower. She pined away with thinking. And with a pale and sickly melancholy, she sat like the figure of Patience on a tombstone, smiling at her grief. Wasn't this love indeed? We men may say more and swear more, but indeed we are insincere. For we always make great vows, but love very little.

Duke And did your sister die for her love, my boy?

Viola I am the only daughter in my father's house—and the only brother too—and yet I don't know. Sir, shall I go to this lady?

Duke Yes, that's the idea. Go to her quickly. Give her this jewel. Say that my love cannot yield and will accept no denial.

[*The* **Duke** *and* **Viola** *exit*]

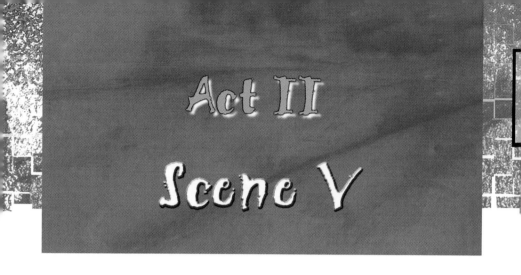

Act II

Scene V

Olivia's Garden. Enter **Sir Toby Belch, Sir Andrew Aguecheek,** *and* **Fabian.**

Sir Toby Come thy ways, Signior Fabian.

Fabian Nay, I'll come; if I lose a scruple of this sport, let me be boiled to death with melancholy.

Sir Toby Would'st thou not be glad to have the niggardly,
5 rascally sheep-biter come by some notable shame?

Fabian I would exult, man; you know he brought me out o' favour with my lady about a bear-baiting here.

Sir Toby To anger him we'll have the bear again, and we will fool him black and blue; shall we not, Sir Andrew?

10 **Sir Andrew** An we do not, it is pity of our lives.

[*Enter* **Maria**]

Sir Toby Here comes the little villain. How now, my metal of India?

Maria Get ye all three into the box-tree. Malvolio's coming down this walk; he has been yonder i' the sun, practising
15 behaviour to his own shadow this half hour. Observe him, for the love of mockery; for I know this letter will make a contemplative idiot of him. Close, in the name of jesting! Lie

Olivia's garden. **Sir Toby, Sir Andrew,** *and* **Fabian** *enter.*

Sir Toby Come along, Mister Fabian.

Fabian I'll come, all right. If I miss the tiniest bit of this sport, may I be boiled to death with misery!

Sir Toby Wouldn't you be glad to have the stingy, rascally, nasty sneak be thoroughly shamed?

Fabian I would rejoice, man. You know that he got me into trouble with my lady over the bear-baiting here.

Sir Toby We'll have the bear back again to anger him. And we will mock him till he's black and blue, won't we, Sir Andrew?

Sir Andrew If we don't, life won't be worth living!

[**Maria** *enters*]

Sir Toby Here comes the little villain. How are things, my precious?

Maria All three of you hide behind the hedge. Malvolio's coming down this walk. He has been over there in the sun, practicing courtly bows to his own shadow for the past half hour. Watch him, for the love of mockery, because I know this letter will make a day-dreaming idiot of him. Keep hidden, in the name of jesting! [*The men hide themselves*] Lie there,

thou there; [*She throws down a letter*] for here comes the
trout that must be caught with tickling.

[*Exit*]

[*Enter* **Malvolio**]

20 **Malvolio** 'Tis but fortune; all is fortune. Maria once told me
she did affect me; and I have heard herself come thus near,
that, should she fancy, it should be one of my complexion.
Besides, she uses me with a more exalted respect than any
one else that follows her. What should I think on't?

25 **Sir Toby** Here's an overweening rogue!

Fabian O, peace! Contemplation makes a rare turkey-cock of
him; how he jets under his advanced plumes!

Sir Andrew 'Slight, I could so beat the rogue!

Sir Toby Peace! I say!

30 **Malvolio** To be Count Malvolio!

Sir Toby Ah, rogue!

Sir Andrew Pistol him, pistol him.

Sir Toby Peace! peace!

Malvolio There is example for 't; the lady of the Strachy
35 married the yeoman of the wardrobe.

Sir Andrew Fie on him, Jezebel!

Fabian O! peace! now he's deeply in; look how imagination
blows him.

Malvolio Having been three months married to her, sitting
40 in my state, –

letter. [*She drops the letter on the path*] For here comes the trout that must be caught by tickling with this lure.

[**Maria** *exits*]

[**Malvolio** *enters*]

Malvolio   It's only chance; everything is matter of chance. Maria once told me that Olivia was fond of me. And I have heard her say this much, that if she did fall in love, it would be with someone like me. Besides, she treats me with greater respect than anyone else in her service. What should I make of all this?

Sir Toby   [*to* **Sir Andrew** *and* **Fabian**]   Here's a conceited rogue!

Fabian   Hush! Day-dreaming makes a rare peacock of him. Look how he struts under his spread plumes!

Sir Andrew   By God, I could give the rogue such a beating!

Sir Toby   Quiet, I say!

Malvolio   To be Count Malvolio.

Sir Toby   Ah, rogue!

Sir Andrew   Shoot him! Shoot him!

Sir Toby   Quiet! Quiet!

Malvolio   There's precedent for it. The lady of Strachy married her servant in charge of the wardrobe.

Sir Andrew   [*absurdly misapplying to* **Malvolio** *the name of a notorious biblical queen*]   Curse him, the Jezebel!

Fabian   Oh, quiet! He's really into it now. Look how his imagination puffs him up.

Malvolio   Having been three months married to her, sitting in my chair of state—

Sir Toby O! for a stone-bow, to hit him in the eye.

Malvolio Calling my officers about me, in my branched velvet gown; having come from a day-bed, where I have left Olivia sleeping, –

45 **Sir Toby** Fire and brimstone!

Fabian O, peace! peace!

Malvolio And then to have the humour of state; and after a demure travel of regard, telling them I know my place, as I would they should do theirs, to ask for my kinsman Toby, –

50 **Sir Toby** Bolts and shackles!

Fabian O, peace, peace, peace! Now, now.

Malvolio Seven of my people, with an obedient start, make out for him. I frown the while, and perchance wind up my watch, or play with my – some rich jewel. Toby approaches,
55 curtsies there to me, –

Sir Toby Shall this fellow live?

Fabian Though our silence be drawn from us with cars, yet peace!

Malvolio I extend my hand to him thus, quenching my
60 familiar smile with an austere regard of control, –

Sir Toby And does not Toby take you a blow o' the lips then?

Malvolio Saying, 'Cousin Toby, my fortunes, having cast me on your niece, give me this prerogative of speech,' –

65 **Sir Toby** What, what?

Malvolio 'You must amend your drunkenness.'

Sir Toby Oh, for a slingshot, to hit him in the eye!

Malvolio I call my household staff around me. Dressed in my ornate velvet gown, having come from a daybed, where I left Olivia sleeping—

Sir Toby Fire and brimstone!

Fabian Oh, quiet! Quiet!

Malvolio And then I adopt a grand manner; and after letting my gaze travel solemnly over my staff—thus indicating to them that I know my place as I would expect them to know theirs—I call for my kinsman Toby—

Sir Toby Bolts and shackles!

Fabian Oh, quiet, quiet, quiet! Now, now.

Malvolio Seven of my servants, in obedient haste, go to seek him. I frown meanwhile, and perhaps wind up my watch, or play with my [*he touches his steward's chain and then remembers he would no longer be wearing it*]—some rich jewel. Toby approaches; bows to me there—

Sir Toby Shall this fellow be allowed to live?

Fabian Even if our silence is drawn from us by force, we still must be quiet!

Malvolio [*stretching out his hand in a proud manner*] I extend my hand to him so, replacing my usual smile with a look of stern authority—

Sir Toby And does not Sir Toby hit you in the mouth then?

Malvolio Saying, "Cousin Toby, my fortunes, having bestowed me on your niece, give me the right to speak"—

Sir Toby What? What?

Malvolio "You must remedy your drunkenness."

Sir Toby Out, scab!

Fabian Nay, patience, or we break the sinews of our plot.

70 **Malvolio** 'Besides, you waste the treasure of your time with a foolish knight,' –

Sir Andrew That's me, I warrant you.

Malvolio 'One Sir Andrew,' –

Sir Andrew I knew't was I; for many do call me fool.

Malvolio [*Seeing the letter*] What employment have we here?

75 **Fabian** Now is the woodcock near the gin. — Metaphor

Sir Toby O, peace! and the spirit of humours intimate reading aloud to him!

Malvolio By my life, this is my lady's hand! These be her very C's, her U's and her T's; and thus makes she her great
80 P's. It is, in contempt of question, her hand.

Sir Andrew Her C's, her U's and her T's; why that?

Malvolio [*Reading*] To the unknown beloved, this, and my good wishes; Her very phrases! By your leave, wax. [*He opens the letter*] Soft! and the impressure her Lucrece, with which
85 she uses to seal; 'tis my lady. To whom should this be?

Fabian This wins him, liver and all.

Malvolio [*Reading*] Jove knows I love;
But who?
Lips, do not move:
90 No man must know.
'No man must know.' What follows? The number's altered!
'No man must know.' If this should be thee, Malvolio?

Sir Toby Marry, hang thee, brock!

Sir Toby Away, you scab!

Fabian No! Have patience or you'll ruin our plot.

Malvolio "Besides, you waste your precious time with a foolish knight"—

Sir Andrew That's me, I'll guarantee you.

Malvolio —"one Sir Andrew"—

Sir Andrew I knew it was me, for many people call me a fool.

Malvolio [*picking up the letter*] What do we have here?

Fabian Now the bird is near the trap.

Sir Toby Oh, quiet, and may he have the impulse to read it aloud!

Malvolio By my life, this is my lady's handwriting! These are her exact *C*'s, her *U*'s, and her *T*'s. And this is how she makes her great *P*'s. It is, beyond question, her handwriting.

Sir Andrew Her *C*'s, her *U*'s, and her *T*'s. Why does he say that?

Malvolio [*reading*] "To the unknown beloved, this letter, and my good wishes"—her style of expression! [*He breaks the letter's wax seal*] With your permission, wax. Wait a moment! The impression in the wax is the figure Lucretia, which she always uses to seal letters. It's my lady's letter. To whom has it been sent?

Fabian This will convince him, heart and soul!

Malvolio [*reads*]
    "God knows I love,
      But who?
    Lips do not move,
    No man must know."
"No man must know." What comes next? The meter changes.
"No man must know." What if this should be you, Malvolio?

Sir Toby May you be hanged indeed, stinker!

Malvolio [*Reading*] I may command where I adore;
95   But silence, like a Lucrece knife,
                     With bloodless stroke my heart doth
                        gore:
                     M, O, A, I, doth sway my life.

Fabian A fustian riddle!

100 **Sir Toby** Excellent wench, say I.

Malvolio 'M, O, A, I, doth sway my life.' Nay, but first, let me see, let me see, let me see.

Fabian What a dish o' poison has she dressed him!

Sir Toby And with what wing the staniel checks at it!

105 **Malvolio** 'I may command where I adore.' Why, she may command me; I serve her: she is my lady. Why, this is evident to any formal capacity; and there is no obstruction in this. And the end, – What should that alphabetical position portend? If I could make that resemble something in
110 me – softly! *M, O, A, I,* –

Sir Toby O! ay, make up that; he is now at a cold scent.

Fabian Sowter will cry upon't, for all this, though it be as rank as a fox.

Malvolio *M,* Malvolio; *M,* why, that begins my name!

115 **Fabian** Did not I say he would work it out? The cur is excellent at faults.

Malvolio *M,* – but then there is no consonancy in the sequel; that suffers under probation; *A* should follow, but *O* does.

Fabian And *O* shall end, I hope.

120 **Sir Toby** Ay, or I'll cudgel him, and make him cry *O!*

Malvolio And then *I* comes behind.

Malvolio [*reads*]
    "I may command where I adore,
        But silence, like Lucretia's knife,
    With bloodless wound my heart does gore;
        M. O. A. I. does sway my life."

Fabian What a silly riddle!

Sir Toby Excellent lass, say I!

Malvolio "M. O. A. I. does sway my life." Yes, but first let me see, let me see, let me see.

Fabian What a dish of poison she's prepared for him!

Sir Toby And with what speed the hawk takes the bait!

Malvolio "I may command where I adore." Why, she may command me. I serve her; she is my lady. Why this is obvious to anyone of normal intelligence. There is no difficulty in this. And the last part—what does that arrangement of letters mean? If I could make that relate to something in me! Wait a moment! M. O. A. I.—

Sir Toby [*echoing the sounds of O and I*] Oh, ay, work that out. He's lost the scent.

Fabian This bungling bloodhound will follow this false scent, although it stinks like a fox.

Malvolio *M*—Malvolio. *M*—why that begins my name.

Fabian Didn't I say he would work it out? The dog is good at false scents.

Malvolio *M*—but then there is no consistency in the following letter that stands up to a test. *A* should follow, but *O* does.

Fabian And an *O* [*meaning a hangman's noose*] shall be his end, I hope.

Sir Toby Yes, or I'll beat him, and make him cry *O!*

Malvolio And then *I* comes behind.

Fabian Ay, an you had any eye behind you, you might see
more detraction at your heels than fortunes before you.

Malvolio *M, O, A, I;* this simulation is not as the former; and
125 yet, to crush this a little, it would bow to me, for every one
of these letters are in my name. Soft! here follows prose.
[*Reading*] 'If this fall into thy hand, revolve! In my stars I am
above thee; but be not afraid of greatness; some are born
great, some achieve greatness, and some have greatness
130 thrust upon them. Thy Fates open their hands; let thy blood
and spirit embrace them, and to inure thyself to what thou
art like to be, cast thy humble slough and appear fresh. Be
opposite with a kinsman, surly with servants; let thy tongue
tang arguments of state; put thyself into the trick of
135 singularity: she thus advises thee that sighs for thee.
Remember who commended thy yellow stockings, and
wished to see thee ever cross-gartered; I say, remember. Go
to, thou art made if thou desirest to be so; if not, let me see
thee a steward still, the fellow of servants, and not worthy to
140 touch Fortune's fingers. Farewell. She that would alter
services with thee,

The Fortunate-Unhappy'

Daylight and champain discovers not more. This is open. I
will be proud, I will read politic authors, I will baffle Sir
145 Toby, I will wash off gross acquaintance, I will be point-
devise the very man. I do not now fool myself, to let
imagination jade me; for every reason excites to this, that my
lady loves me. She did commend my yellow stockings of late;
she did praise my leg being cross-gartered; and in this she
150 manifests herself to my love, and with a kind of injunction
drives me to these habits of her liking. I thank my stars I am
happy. I will be strange, stout, in yellow stockings, and
cross-gartered, even with the swiftness of putting on. Jove
and my stars be praised! Here is yet a postscript.
155 [*Reading*] 'Thou canst not choose but know who I am. If thou
entertainest my love, let it appear in thy smiling; thy smile

Fabian Yes, if you had any "eye" behind you, you might see more abuse at your back than good fortune in front of you.

Malvolio M. O. A. I. This puzzle is not as clear as the first. But if I force it a little, it would relate to me, for every one of these letters is in my name. Wait a moment. Prose follows next. [*He reads*] "If this falls into your hands, consider. In my rank I am above you, but do not be afraid of greatness. Some are born great; some achieve greatness; and some have greatness thrust upon them. Fate offers a help to you; embrace it with your heart and soul. To prepare yourself for what you are likely to be, cast off your humble manner and appear new. Be quarrelsome with a certain kinsman, and surly with the servants. Speak forthrightly about important matters; be eccentric. She who sighs for you gives you this advice. Remember who praised your yellow stockings and wished to see you always cross-gartered. Remember, I say. Look here: you are certain of success if you want to be. If not, let me see you a steward always, the equal of servants, and unworthy to grasp Fortune's hand. Farewell. She who would be your servant,

The Fortunate-Unhappy."

Daylight and open country couldn't be clearer! This is perfectly plain. I will be proud. I will read serious writers. I will treat Sir Toby with disdain. I will rid myself of low companions. I will be exactly the man she wants in every detail. I am not fooling myself now, or letting my imagination trick me. For every piece of evidence prompts this conclusion: my lady loves me. She did lately praise my yellow stockings; she did praise the look of my cross-gartered legs. And in this letter, she shows her love by giving me a kind of order to force me to dress as she likes. I thank my lucky stars that I am so fortunate. I will be aloof, proud, in yellow stockings, and cross-gartered, as quickly as I can put them on. God and my stars be praised! Here's a postcript. [*Reads*] "You cannot help but know who I am. If you accept my love, let it show in your smiling. Your smiles are very

becomes thee well; therefore in my presence still smile, dear
my sweet, I prithee.'
160   Jove, I thank thee. I will smile; I will do everything that thou
wilt have me.

[Exit]

Fabian   I will not give my part of this sport for a pension of
thousands to be paid from the Sophy.

Sir Toby   I could marry this wench for this device.

Sir Andrew   So could I too.

165   **Sir Toby**   And ask no other dowry with her but such another
jest.

Sir Andrew   Nor I neither.

Fabian   Here comes my noble gull-catcher.

[*Enter* **Maria**]

Sir Toby   Wilt thou set thy foot o' my neck?

170   **Sir Andrew**   Or o' mine either?

Sir Toby   Shall I play my freedom at tray-trip, and become
thy bondslave?

Sir Andrew   I' faith, or I either?

Sir Toby   Why, thou hast put him in such a dream, that
175   when the image of it leaves him he must run mad.

Maria   Nay, but say true; does it work upon him?

Sir Toby   Like aqua-vitae with a midwife.

Maria   If you will then see the fruits of the sport, mark his
first approach before my lady; he will come to her in yellow
180   stockings, and 'tis a colour she abhors; and cross-gartered, a
fashion she detests; and he will smile upon her, which will

attractive. Therefore, in my presence always smile, my dear sweetheart, I beg you." I thank heaven. I will smile. I will do everything that you want me to do.

[**Malvolio** *exits*]

Fabian I would not give up my share in this jest for a pension of a thousand pounds to be paid by the Shah of Persia!

Sir Toby And I could marry the lass for this trick.

Sir Andrew So could I too.

Sir Toby And ask no other dowry from her than another such jest.

Sir Andrew Nor I neither.

Fabian Here comes our noble trickster!

[**Maria** *enters*]

Sir Toby Will you place your foot on my neck?

Sir Andrew Or on mine too?

Sir Toby Shall I gamble at dice with you for my freedom, and become your slave?

Sir Andrew Indeed, and shall I too?

Sir Toby Why, you have put him in such a dream, that when he awakes from it he will go mad.

Maria No, tell the truth, did it have an effect on him?

Sir Toby Like brandy on a midwife.

Maria Then if you want to see the results of the jest, watch when he first comes to see to my lady. He will come to her in yellow stockings, and that's a color she hates; and cross-gartered, which is a fashion she detests. And he will smile at

now be so unsuitable to her disposition, being addicted to a melancholy as she is, that it cannot but turn him into a notable contempt. If you will see it, follow me.

185 **Sir Toby** To the gates of Tartar, thou most excellent devil of wit.

Sir Andrew I'll make one too.

[*Exeunt*]

her, which is now so inappropriate to her mood, being given to sorrow as she is, that it must bring him into great disgrace. If you want to see it, follow me.

Sir Toby To the gates of hell, you most excellent devil of cunning!

Sir Andrew I'll go along too.

[*They exit*]

Comprehension   Check What You Know

1. Who is Sebastian? What is the relationship between him and Antonio?

2. Why is Viola surprised when Malvolio returns a ring to her? What does Viola think that returning the ring says about Olivia?

3. Why does Malvolio interrupt Toby, Andrew, and Feste? What is their response to Malvolio's statements? What warning does Malvolio give to Maria?

4. What will Maria include in the letter to Malvolio?

5. In Scene 4, the Duke tells Viola/Cesario he thinks that Cesario has fallen in love with someone. How does Viola tell Orsino that indeed she does love someone?

6. Orsino and Viola/Cesario argue about Olivia. Why does Orsino think that Olivia will ultimately give in? What is Viola's response?

7. When Malvolio is walking in the garden, he ponders on the possibility that Olivia might favor him. Why does he think that he might marry her?

8. Why are Toby, Andrew, and Fabian outraged by Malvolio's comments?

9. What things in the letter convince Malvolio that it is from Olivia and talks about him? What instructions are included in the letter?

10. How will Sir Toby, Sir Andrew, Fabian, and Maria know that their scheme has worked?

Activities & Role-Playing   Classes or Book Clubs

Words of Passion In Scene 4, Orsino and Viola/Cesario argue about whether Orsino should continue to pursue Olivia. Working with a partner, take on one role or the other and read the lines back and forth. Are the players angry? Pleading? Sorrowful? Desperate? Menacing? Does Cesario feel he is running a

Peter Webster as Orsino and Kelly McGillis as Viola in The Shakespeare Theater's 1989 production of *Twelfth Night* directed by Michael Kahn. Photo by Joan Marcus.

risk by challenging the Duke? Does the Duke feel at ease with Cesario and treat him as an equal?

Sing a Song Review Feste's song in Act 2. What is its basic message? Why does he choose this particular song for this audience? What do you learn about Toby and Andrew from their responses to the song? Then consider this: Just because a song has sad lyrics, it doesn't have to be sung in a sad style. Many folk songs have a lilting rhythm, even though the story they tell is often brutal and tragic. How should this song be sung? Consider the mood of the characters who are listening. How does the song fit in with the theme of love that fills the play?

Discussion Classes or Book Clubs

1. Maria is sure that her practical joke will fool Malvolio. Study her conversation with Sir Toby and Sir Andrew in Scene 3, lines 119–159. Then read over Malvolio's soliloquy in the garden in Scene 5. What is it about Malvolio's character that makes it possible to fool him so completely?

2. Read the short speech that Feste makes before he leaves Duke Orsino (Scene 4, lines 77–82). Why does Feste compare the Duke to an opal and taffeta, then say that he wishes such men were put to sea?

3. Why does the Duke continue to court Olivia? What is it about her that he finds so desirable? Compare his behavior with the behavior of Cesario's "sister." What are the differences? Which love seems more genuine? Why?

Suggestions for Writing Improve Your Skills

1. Pretend you are a servant who attends Olivia. Write a letter to a friend describing some of the goings-on. Describe the main characters. Explain the dilemmas that surround them, and speculate about what will happen next.

2. Viola/Cesario is in a fix—the "return of the ring" has indicated that Olivia is falling for Cesario. Pretend you are Viola, and write an entry in your diary, analyzing what has happened. Explain how you feel about the Duke and about Olivia. What can you do to get yourself out of this mess?

3. Make a list of the people Malvolio has irritated in Acts 1 and 2, and add notes about what he did. Then write a letter to Olivia to explain what's going on. Discuss Malvolio's character and how it has caused problems.

4. Viola says she loves the Duke, but she still carries Orsino's messages to Olivia and sincerely pleads his case with her. Analyze her speeches and her conversations with herself. Then write a short explanation of her actions.

All the World's a Stage Introduction

Ooops! Viola is in a bit of a fix. To make herself safe, she disguised herself as a young man and joined the court of Duke Orsino—only to be asked to court another woman, Olivia, in the Duke's name while having fallen in love with the Duke herself. To make things even more complicated, when Viola/Cesario tried to convince Olivia of the Duke's devotion, Viola described his passion so well that Olivia instead fell in love with Cesario. What's a woman pretending to be a man supposed to do?

Conflict is also brewing in Illyria. Malvolio, Olivia's straight-laced steward, feels that everyone else should be like him. He confronted Olivia's uncle, Sir Toby, and his friend, Sir Andrew, who were having a great time carousing through the days and nights—often too loudly for Malvolio's sense of propriety. He also criticized Feste, the fool, for having a frivolous view of everything—which is, of course, Feste's job. Finally, Malvolio threatened to have Maria, Olivia's maid, expelled from the house if she can't control Toby and Andrew. Everyone wants revenge against Malvolio. And they're definitely going to get it.

What's in a Name? Characters

Throughout the play several people describe Malvolio as a *gull*. At the end of Act 2, Fabian calls Maria a "gull-catcher." A gull is a person who is easy to make the butt of a joke or a scheme—a person who is *gullible*. In a modern story, a gull might be a "mark," a person who is easy to con. For instance, the mark is offered the chance to make millions on an oil well. If the mark is conceited, lazy, or greedy enough, the con will work.

In Act 2, you saw the things in Malvolio's character that make him a perfect gull. Self-centered and ambitious, he is so sure he's superior that even before he reads the letter he believes it would be totally logical that Olivia would choose him over all others. His motives are clear. He doesn't want Olivia because he loves her—he wants her because then he would have power over everyone, including Sir Toby. Because he's so sure of his importance, everyone is gleefully waiting for him to make a fool of himself with Olivia.

COME WHAT MAY Things to Watch For

Everyone can imagine the "perfect love," and the characters in *Twelfth Night* are no exception. In Acts 1 and 2 Orsino talked more about his own agony over Olivia than he did about Olivia herself. But not everyone in the play is so romantic. In Act 3, you will have the chance to compare the ways that Olivia and Viola look at expressions of love. Is anger or pity an expression of love? Is jealousy? Is possessiveness?

The disagreements between Orsino, Olivia, and Viola are one way that Shakespeare explores some of the silliness of romantic love. He uses Sir Toby to show how a clever man can use romantic notions about love to gull someone. Watch to see how he and Fabian use Sir Andrew's notions to keep him at the castle and to provoke some fun between him and Viola/Cesario.

All Our Yesterdays Historical and Social Context

All through *Twelfth Night* various characters act as if they're slightly insane or under someone's spell—that's one source of the humor of the play. But insanity and possession were not laughing matters in Shakespeare's England. The main hospital for the mentally disturbed was Saint Mary of Bethlehem, called Bedlam for short. If a person was suffering seriously from a mental disease, people believed he or she was possessed by evil spirits. The sufferer was then imprisoned in a dark place, sometimes for long periods of time. The darkness was supposed to drive out the evil spirits.

The Play's the Thing Staging

The actors in Shakespeare's plays wore contemporary dress. Costume wasn't used to distinguish between different groups. The people from Illyria would not dress any differently than Viola or Sebastian. But in *Twelfth Night*, one costume item would have received special attention: Malvolio's *cross-gartering*. In Elizabethan times stockings were held in place near the knee with a strap called a garter. Sometimes people wrapped their garters to form a criss-cross design—they were cross-gartered. Many people in the audience would have found cross-gartering as silly as Olivia does.

My Words Fly Up Language

In Act 2, when Viola/Cesario told Duke Orsino that her father had a daughter who loved a man, just as Cesario might love the Duke if Cesario were a woman, Shakespeare is using a writing technique called *irony*. In irony a person says one thing but means the opposite. If a friend tells you that geography is really fun and you reply "Right," even though you don't agree, you are being ironic.

In Act 3 the irony grows and grows. Sometimes one person knows the truth and the other does not, as when Viola/Cesario says that no woman will ever rule her heart except Viola/Cesario herself. At other times the irony is easy to see, as when Sir Toby praises a letter that Sir Andrew has written.

Another aspect of language arises in Act 3. The words say that people become opportunities for jokes, as when Viola asks Feste where he lives. Or they become an opportunity for a game, as when Sir Andrew reacts to seeing Olivia and Cesario talking together in the garden.

Act III

Scene I

Olivia's Garden. Enter **Viola** *and* **Feste** *with a tabor.*

Viola Save thee, friend, and thy music! Dost thou live by thy
tabor?

Feste No, sir, I live by the church.

Viola Art thou a churchman?

5 **Feste** No such matter, sir; I do live by the church, for I do
live at my house, and my house doth stand by the church.

Viola So thou mayest say, the king lies by a beggar if a beggar
dwell near him; or, the church stands by thy tabor, if thy
tabor stand by the church.

10 **Feste** You have said, sir. To see this age! A sentence is but a
cheveril glove to a good wit; how quickly the wrong side
may be turned outward!

Viola Nay, that's certain; they that dally nicely with words
may quickly make them wanton.

15 **Feste** I would therefore my sister had no name, sir.

Viola Why, man?

Feste Why, sir, her name's a word; and to dally with that
word might make my sister wanton. But indeed words are
very rascals since bonds disgraced them.

20 **Viola** Thy reason, man?

Olivia's garden. **Viola** *and* **Feste,** *who is carrying a small drum, enter.*

Viola God save you, friend, and your music. Do you live by your drum?

Feste No, sir, I live by the church.

Viola Are you a churchman?

Feste Not at all, sir. I live by the church because I live in my house, and my house stands near the church.

Viola So you might say that the king sleeps beside a beggar if a beggar lives near him. Or that the church stands by your drum if your drum is near the church.

Feste That's your opinion, sir. Look at this age! Any statement is just like a kidskin glove to a clever mind. How quickly it can be turned inside out!

Viola Yes, that's true. People that play around with words can quickly make them seem indecent.

Feste I would therefore prefer that my sister had no name.

Viola Why, man?

Feste Why, sir, her name is a word. And to play around with the word might make my sister indecent. But indeed, words have been false since people had to swear they were true.

Viola Your reason, man?

Feste Troth, sir, I can yield you none without words; and words are grown so false, I am loath to prove reason with them.

Viola I warrant thou art a merry fellow, and carest for
25   nothing.

Feste Not so, sir; I do care for something; but in my conscience, sir, I do not care for you; if that be to care for nothing, sir, I would it would make you invisible.

Viola Art not thou the Lady Olivia's fool?

30 **Feste** No, indeed, sir; the Lady Olivia has no folly; she will keep no fool, sir, till she be married; and fools are as like husbands as pilchards are to herrings – the husband's the bigger. I am indeed not her fool, but her corrupter of words.

Viola I saw thee late at the Count Orsino's.

35 **Feste** Foolery, sir, does walk about the orb like the sun: it shines everywhere. I would be sorry, sir, but the fool should be as oft with your master as with my mistress. I think I saw your wisdom there.

Viola Nay, an thou pass upon me, I'll no more with thee.
40   Hold, there's expenses for thee.

Feste Now Jove, in his next commodity of hair, send thee a beard!

Viola By my troth, I'll tell thee, I am almost sick for one, though I would not have it grow on my chin. Is thy lady
45   within?

Feste Would not a pair of these have bred, sir?

Viola Yes, being kept together and put to use.

Feste I would play Lord Pandarus of Phrygia, sir, to bring a Cressida to this Troilus.

Feste Truly, sir, I can give you none without words, and words have become so unreliable that I am reluctant to prove my case with them.

Viola I guarantee that you are a merry fellow and care for nothing.

Feste That's not so, sir. I do care for something. But to be honest, sir, I don't care for you. If that means I care for nothing, I wish it would make you invisible.

Viola Aren't you the Lady Olivia's fool?

Feste No indeed, sir. The Lady Olivia has no folly. She won't keep a fool, sir, until she is married. And fools are as like husbands as sardines are like herrings—the husband's the bigger one. Indeed, I'm not her fool but her corrupter of words.

Viola I saw you recently at the Count Orsino's.

Feste Foolery, sir, moves around the earth like the sun; it shines everywhere. I would be sorry, sir, if folly should not be as often with your master as with my mistress. I think I saw your wise self there.

Viola No, if you're going to pass judgment on me, I won't stay with you. Hold on, here's expense money for you. [*She gives him a coin*]

Feste May God, in his next supply of hair, send you a beard!

Viola Truly, I'll tell you I long for one— [*To herself*] although I would not have it grow on my chin. [*To Feste*] Is your lady inside?

Feste [*holding up the coin she gave him*] Wouldn't a pair of these coins breed more, sir?

Viola Yes, if they were kept together and put to use.

Feste I would like to play the go-between to bring another lover to this one. [*He holds up his coin*]

50 **Viola** I understand you, sir; 'tis well begged.

Feste The matter, I hope, is not great, sir, begging but a beggar;
Cressida was a beggar. My lady is within, sir. I will construe
to them whence you come; who you are and what you
would are out of my welkin; I might say 'element', but the
55   word is overworn.

[*Exit*]

Viola This fellow's wise enough to play the fool,
And to do that well craves a kind of wit;
He must observe their mood on whom he jests,
The quality of persons, and the time,
60   Not, like the haggard, check at every feather
That comes before his eye. This is a practice
As full of labour as a wise man's art,
For folly that he wisely shows is fit;
But wise men, folly-fall'n, quite taint their wit.

[*Enter* **Sir Toby Belch** *and* **Sir Andrew Aguecheek**]

65 **Sir Toby** Save you, gentleman.

Viola And you, sir.

Sir Andrew Dieu vous garde, monsieur.

Viola Et vous aussi; votre serviteur.

Sir Andrew I hope, sir, you are; and I am yours.

70 **Sir Toby** Will you encounter the house? My niece is desirous
you should enter, if your trade be to her.

Viola I understand you, sir. [*She gives him another coin*]
You've begged well.

Feste I hope it's no great thing, sir, for a beggar to beg. A lover
is a beggar. My lady is within, sir. I will explain to my lady
and her servants from where you come. Who you are and
what you want are out of my sphere—I could say "element,"
but the word is overused. [*He leaves*]

Viola This fellow is wise enough to be a jester. And to do that
well requires a kind of cleverness. He must observe the
mood of those for whom he jests, as well as the characters of
people and occasions. And like an untrained hawk he must
strike at every target he sees. This is an exercise of skill as
difficult as any wise man's skill. For the folly that he carefully
cultivates is appropriate. But wise men, when they fall into
foolishness, bring discredit to their intelligence.

[**Sir Toby** *and* **Sir Andrew** *enter*]

Sir Toby God save you, gentleman.

Viola And you too, sir.

Sir Andrew [*repeating Sir Toby's greeting, this time in French*]
Dieu vous garde, monsieur.

Viola *Et vous aussi; votre serviteur.* [*"And you too, sir; (I am)
your servant."*]

Sir Andrew [*unable to respond in French to Viola's fluency*] I
hope you are, sir; and I am yours.

Sir Toby Will you approach the house, sir? My niece desires
you should enter, if your business is with her.

Viola I am bound to your niece, sir; I mean, she is the list of
my voyage.

Sir Toby Taste your legs, sir; put them to motion.

75 **Viola** My legs do better under-stand me, sir, than I
understand what you mean by bidding me taste my legs.

Sir Toby I mean, to go, sir, to enter.

Viola I will answer you with gait and entrance. But we are
prevented.

[*Enter* **Olivia** *and* **Maria**]

80 Most excellent accomplished lady, the heavens rain odours
on you!

Sir Andrew The youth's a rare courtier. 'Rain odours!' Well.

Viola My matter hath no voice, lady, but to your own most
pregnant and vouchsafed ear.

85 **Sir Andrew** 'Odours', 'pregnant', and 'vouchsafed'; I'll get
'em all three all ready.

Olivia Let the garden door be shut, and leave me to my
hearing.

[*Exeunt* **Sir Toby, Sir Andrew,** *and* **Maria**]

Give me your hand, sir.

90 **Viola** My duty, madam, and most humble service.

Olivia What is your name?

Viola Cesario is your servant's name, fair princess.

Olivia My servant, sir! 'Twas never merry world
Since lowly feigning was called compliment.
95 You're servant to the Count Orsino, youth.

Viola I am bound to your niece; I mean, she is the purpose of my journey.

Sir Toby Test your legs, sir. Put them in motion.

Viola My legs "under stand" me better, sir, than I understand what you mean by directing me to "test my legs."

Sir Toby I mean go in, sir; enter.

Viola I will answer with my gait and your entrance [*punning on* gate]—But we are anticipated.

[**Olivia** *and* **Maria** *enter*]

Most excellent and accomplished lady, may the heavens rain odors on you!

Sir Andrew That youth's a splendid courtier. "Rain odors"—well.

Viola My message cannot be spoken, lady, but to your own pregnant [*"receptive"*] and vouchsafed [*"offered"*] ear.

Sir Andrew "Odors," "pregnant," and "vouchsafed." I must remember to use them.

Olivia [*to* **Maria**] Shut the garden door and leave me alone to hear him. [**Sir Toby, Sir Andrew,** *and* **Maria** *leave*] Give me your hand, sir.

Viola I am your most dutiful and humble servant, madam.

Olivia What is your name?

Viola Cesario is your servant's name, fair princess.

Olivia My servant, sir? The world has grown worse if false humility is taken for compliment. You're Count Orsino's servant, youth.

Viola And he is yours, and his must needs be yours;
Your servant's servant is your servant, madam.

Olivia For him, I think not on him; for his thoughts,
Would they were blanks rather than filled with me!

100 **Viola** Madam, I come to whet your gentle thoughts
On his behalf.

Olivia   O! by your leave, I pray you,
I bade you never speak again of him;
But, would you undertake another suit,
105 I had rather hear you to solicit that
Than music from the spheres.

Viola   Dear lady, –

Olivia Give me leave, beseech you. I did send,
After the last enchantment you did here,
110 A ring in chase of you; so did I abuse
Myself, my servant, and, I fear me, you;
Under your hard construction must I sit,
To force that on you, in a shameful cunning,
Which you knew none of yours, what might you think?
115 Have you not set mine honour at the stake,
And baited it with all the unmuzzled thoughts
That tyrannous heart can think?
To one of your receiving, enough is shown;
A cypress, not a bosom, hides my heart.
120 So, let me hear you speak.

Viola I pity you.

Olivia   That's a degree to love.

Viola No, not a grize; for 'tis a vulgar proof
That very oft we pity enemies.

125 **Olivia** Why, then, methinks 'tis time to smile again.
O world! how apt the poor are to be proud.
If one should be a prey, how much the better
To fall before the lion than the wolf!

Viola And he is your servant, and his must therefore be yours. Your servant's servant is *your* servant, madam.

Olivia As for him, I don't think about him. As for his thoughts, I wish they were blanks, rather than filled with me.

Viola Madam, I come to arouse your gentle thoughts on his behalf.

Olivia Oh, please let me stop you. I ordered you to never speak of him. But, if you will begin courting me again, I would rather listen to *your* wooing than heavenly music.

Viola Dear lady—

Olivia Please let me interrupt you. After your last enchanting visit here, I sent a ring in pursuit of you. In this way, I fear that I wronged myself, my servant, and you. I must accept your harsh judgment for forcing on you through a shameful trick something you knew wasn't yours. What must you think? Haven't you tied my honor to the stake and let your heart's cruelest thoughts attack it like vicious dogs? I've said enough. A mere veil, not flesh, hides my heart. So, let me hear you speak.

Viola I pity you.

Olivia That's a step toward love.

Viola No, not a step. For it's a common experience that very often we pity our enemies.

Olivia Well, then, I think it's time to learn to smile again. Oh world! How likely the poor are to be proud! If one must be a victim, how much better to be killed by a lion than a wolf!

Personification

[*Clock strikes*]

The clock upbraids me with the waste of time.
130   Be not afraid, good youth, I will not have you;
And yet, when wit and youth is come to harvest,
Your wife is like to reap a proper man.
There lies your way, due west.

Viola   Then westward-ho!
135   Grace and good disposition attend your ladyship!
You'll nothing, madam, to my lord by me?

Olivia Stay;
I prithee, tell me what thou think'st of me.

Viola That you do think you are not what you are.

140   **Olivia** If I think so, I think the same of you.

Viola Then think you right; I am not what I am.

Don't judge a book by its cover

Olivia I would you were as I would have you be!

Viola Would it be better, madam, than I am?
I wish it might, for now I am your fool.

145   **Olivia** O! what a deal of scorn looks beautiful
In the contempt and anger of his lip.
A murderous guilt shows not itself more soon
Than love that would seem hid; love's night is noon.
Cesario, by the roses of the spring,
150   By maidhood, honour, truth, and every thing,
I love thee so, that, maugre all thy pride,
Nor wit nor reason can my passion hide.
Do not extort thy reasons from this clause,
For that I woo, thou therefore hast no cause;

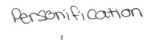

Personification

!

[*A clock strikes*] The clock scolds me for wasting time. Be not afraid, good youth. You're not for me. And yet, when your mind and body are fully matured, your wife is likely to get a fine man. There lies your way, due west.

Viola Then, westward-ho! May your ladyship have God's blessing and peace of mind. You'll have me bring no word to my lord, madam?

Olivia Wait. I beg you, tell me what you think of me.

Viola [*talking in riddles*] That you think you are not what you are. [*"You think you're in love with a man, but you're not."*]

Olivia If I think so, I think the same of you. [*She has interpreted Viola's riddle as meaning, "You think you aren't mad, but you are."*]

Viola Then you think correctly. I am not what I am. [*"I'm not a man."*]

Olivia I wish you were what I want you to be! [*"I want you to be my husband."*]

Viola Would that be better, madam, than what I am? I hope it might be, for now you are making a fool of me!

Olivia [*to herself*] Oh, how beautiful scorn can look when his lips speak anger and contempt! Love that tries to hide itself is revealed sooner than a murderer's guilt. Love's attempt at secrecy is plain to everyone. [*To* **Viola**] Cesario, by the roses of the spring, by maidenhood, honor, truth, and everything else, I love you so much that, in spite of all your pride, neither common sense nor prudence can hide my passion. Don't conclude that, because I woo you, you need not respond. Instead, reason this way: love that is sought is

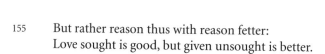

155 But rather reason thus with reason fetter:
Love sought is good, but given unsought is better.

Viola By innocence I swear, and by my youth,
I have one heart, one bosom, and one truth,
And that no woman has; nor never none
160 Shall mistress be of it, save I alone.
And so adieu, good madam; never more
Will I my master's tears to you deplore.

Olivia Yet come again, for thou perhaps may'st move
That heart, which now abhors, to like his love.

[*Exeunt*]

good; but love that is given without being sought is even better.

Viola By innocence and by my youth, I swear that no woman possesses my heart, my soul, and my self, and none ever shall be mistress of them but I alone. And so farewell, good madam. Nevermore will I plead to you over my master's tears.

Olivia But do come again. For perhaps you may make my heart, which now rejects his love, to want it.

[**Olivia** *and* **Viola** *exit*]

Act III

Scene II

Olivia's House. Enter **Sir Toby Belch, Sir Andrew Aguecheek** *and* **Fabian.**

Sir Andrew No, faith, I'll not stay a jot longer.

Sir Toby Thy reason, dear venom; give thy reason.

Fabian You must needs yield your reason, Sir Andrew.

Sir Andrew Marry, I saw your niece do more favours to the
5   count's serving-man than ever she bestowed upon me; I saw't
i' the orchard.

Sir Toby Did she see thee the while, old boy? Tell me that.

Sir Andrew As plain as I see you now.

Fabian This was a great argument of love in her toward you.

10 **Sir Andrew** Slight! will you make an ass o' me?

Fabian I will prove it legitimate, sir, upon the oaths of
judgement and reason.

Sir Toby And they have been grand-jurymen since before
Noah was a sailor.

15 **Fabian** She did show favour to the youth in your sight only
to exasperate you, to awake your dormouse valour, to put
fire in your heart, and brimstone in your liver. You should
then have accosted her, and with some excellent jests, fire-new
from the mint, you should have banged the youth into

A room in Olivia's house. **Sir Toby, Sir Andrew,** *and* **Fabian** *enter.*

Sir Andrew   No, indeed, I'll not stay a moment longer.

Sir Toby   Your reason, my angry friend, give your reason.

Fabian   You must give your reason, Sir Andrew.

Sir Andrew   Well, I saw your niece acting more favorably to the count's servant than she ever has to me. I saw them in the garden.

Sir Toby   Did she see you at the same time, old boy? Tell me that.

Sir Andrew   As plain as I see you now.

Fabian   This is a great proof of her love for you.

Sir Andrew   By God, are you trying to make an ass of me?

Fabian   I'll prove it's true, on the sworn testimony of common sense and reason.

Sir Toby   And they have been accepted as evidence since before Noah was a sailor.

Fabian   She acted favorably to the youth in your sight only to exasperate you, to wake up your sleeping valor, to put fire in your heart and arouse your passions. You should have confronted her boldly then, and with some smart remarks, all brand-new, have struck the young man dumb. This was

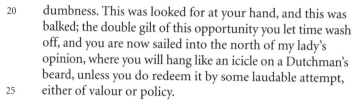

20   dumbness. This was looked for at your hand, and this was
balked; the double gilt of this opportunity you let time wash
off, and you are now sailed into the north of my lady's
opinion, where you will hang like an icicle on a Dutchman's
beard, unless you do redeem it by some laudable attempt,
25   either of valour or policy.

Sir Andrew An't be any way, it must be with valour, for
policy I hate; I had as lief be a Brownist as a politician.

Sir Toby Why then, build me thy fortunes upon the basis of
valour; challenge me the count's youth to fight with him;
30   hurt him in eleven places; my niece shall take note of it;
and assure thyself, there is no lover-broker in the world
can more prevail in man's commendation with woman
than report of valour.

Fabian There is no way but this, Sir Andrew.

35 **Sir Andrew** Will either of you bear me a challenge to him?

Sir Toby Go, write it in a martial hand; be curst and brief; it
is no matter how witty, so it be eloquent and full of
invention; taunt him with the licence of ink; if thou thou'st
him some thrice, it shall not be amiss; and as many lies as
40   will lie in thy sheet of paper, although the sheet were big
enough for the bed of Ware in England, set 'em down; go,
about it. Let there be gall enough in thy ink, though thou
write with a goose-pen, no matter. About it.

Sir Andrew Where shall I find you?

45 **Sir Toby** We'll call thee at the cubiculo; go.

                                    [*Exit* **Sir Andrew**]

Fabian This is a dear manakin to you, Sir Toby.

Sir Toby I have been dear to him, lad; some two thousand
strong or so.

expected from you, and you missed your chance. You let this golden opportunity get away, and now you're out in the cold. There you'll hang like an icicle on a Dutchman's beard, unless you redeem yourself with some praiseworthy effort of either valor or of clever policy.

Sir Andrew If it's going to be any way at all, it must be with valor, for I hate policy. I would as soon be a puritan as a politician.

Sir Toby Why, then, build your fortunes on the basis of valor. Challenge the count's youth to a fight. Hurt him in eleven places. My niece shall hear of it. Be assured, there's no matchmaker in the world that can do a better job of praising a man to a woman than a reputation for valor.

Fabian There is no other way, Sir Andrew.

Sir Andrew Will either of you take my challenge to him?

Sir Toby Go, write it in a bold script. Be fierce and brief. It doesn't matter how clever it is, so long as it's eloquent and inventive. You can insult him safely in writing. It wouldn't be a bad idea if you call him "boy" two or three times. Tell as many lies as will lie in your sheet of paper, even if the sheet were big enough for a bed that slept a dozen. Go, get to work. If there's acid enough in your ink, it doesn't matter if you write with a goose pen. [*He puns on two meanings of goose, "quill" and "foolish."*] Get to work.

Sir Andrew Where will I find you?

Sir Toby We'll call for you at the writing room.

[**Sir Andrew** *leaves*]

Fabian He's a dear puppet in your hands, Sir Toby.

Sir Toby I have been dear to him, lad, some two thousand ducats or so.

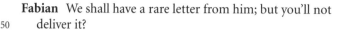

Fabian We shall have a rare letter from him; but you'll not
50   deliver it?

Sir Toby Never trust me, then; and by all means stir on the
youth to an answer. I think oxen and wainropes cannot hale
them together. For Andrew, if he were opened, and you find
so much blood in his liver as will clog the foot of a flea, I'll
55   eat the rest of the anatomy.

Fabian And his opposite, the youth, bears in his visage no
great presage of cruelty.

[*Enter* **Maria**]

Sir Toby Look, where the youngest wren of nine comes.

Maria If you desire the spleen, and will laugh yourselves into
60   stitches, follow me. Yond gull Malvolio is turned to heathen, a
very renegado; for there is no Christian, that means to be
saved by believing rightly, can ever believe such impossible
passages of grossness. He's in yellow stockings!

Sir Toby And cross-gartered?

65 **Maria** Most villainously; like a pedant that keeps a school i'
the church. I have dogged him like his murderer. He does
obey every point of the letter that I dropped to betray him; he
does smile his face into more lines than is in the new map
with the augmentation of the Indies. You have not seen such
70   a thing as 'tis; I can hardly forbear hurling things at him. I
know my lady will strike him; if she do, he'll smile and take't
for a great favour.

Sir Toby Come, bring us, bring us where he is.

[*Exeunt*]

Fabian We'll get a rare letter from him. But you won't deliver it?

Sir Toby If I don't, never trust me again! And I'll do my best to provoke the youth to reply. But I don't think oxen and wagon ropes could drag them together. As for Andrew, if you opened him up and found as much blood in him as would slow the foot of a flea, I'll eat the rest of his remains.

Fabian And his opponent, the youth, has in his face no strong indication of fierceness.

[**Maria** *enters*]

Sir Toby Look, here comes the tiniest wren in the nest!

Maria If you want to laugh yourselves into a fit and be in stitches, follow me. That fool Malvolio has turned heathen and deserted his religion. For no Christian that means to be saved by believing rightly could ever have believed the grossly impossible passages in the letter we left for him. He's in yellow stockings.

Sir Toby And cross-gartered?

Maria Hideously—like a parish schoolmaster. I have stalked him like a murderer. He has obeyed every item of the letter that I dropped to trick him. He smiles his face into more wrinkles than there are lines on the new map of the Indies. You've never seen anything like it! I can hardly keep myself from throwing things at him. I know my lady will hit him. If she does, he'll smile and take it for a great favor.

Sir Toby Come, take us, take us where he is.

[*They exit*]

Act III

Scene III

A Street. Enter **Sebastian** *and* **Antonio.**

Sebastian I would not by my will have troubled you;
But since you make your pleasure of your pains,
I will no further chide you.

Antonio I could not stay behind you; my desire,
5   More sharp than filed steel, did spur me forth;
And not all love to see you, though so much
As might have drawn one to a longer voyage,
But jealousy what might befall your travel,
Being skilless in these parts, which to a stranger,
10   Unguided and unfriended, often prove
Rough and inhospitable; my willing love,
The rather by these arguments of fear,
Set forth in your pursuit.

Sebastian   My kind Antonio,
15   I can no other answer make but thanks,
And thanks, and ever thanks; and oft good turns
Are shuffled off with such uncurrent pay;
But, were my worth, as in my conscience, firm,
You should find better dealing. What's to do?
20   Shall we go see the relics of this town?

Antonio Tomorrow, sir; best first go see your lodging.

Sebastian I am not weary, and 'tis long to night.
I pray you, let us satisfy our eyes
With the memorials and the things of fame
25   That do renown this city.

A street. **Sebastian** *and* **Antonio** *enter.*

Sebastian I would not willingly have troubled you, but since you take pleasure in taking pains, I won't scold you any more.

Antonio I couldn't stay away from you. My desire, sharper than a steel edge, urged me onward. And it wasn't only the desire to see you—though that was great enough to set me off on an even longer journey. But I worried what might happen to you on your travels. You have no knowledge of this country, which to a stranger, with no guide or companion, can often prove rough and unfriendly. My eager love, heightened by these fears for you, set me forth to follow you.

Sebastian My kind Antonio, I can make no other reply but to thank you again and again. Very often, good turns are shrugged off with such worthless payment. But if my wealth were as great as my gratitude to you, you should get a better reward. [*Pause*] What is there to do here? Shall we go see the local sights?

Antonio Tomorrow, sir. First we had better see about your lodging.

Sebastian I'm not weary, and it's a long time until night. Please, let's feast our eyes on the monuments and famous sights for which the city is known.

Antonio   Would you'd pardon me;
I do not without danger walk these streets;
Once, in a sea-fight 'gainst the Count his galleys,
I did some service – of such note, indeed,
30   That were I ta'en here it would scarce be answered.

Sebastian Belike you slew great number of his people.

Antonio The offence is not of such a bloody nature,
Albeit the quality of the time and quarrel
Might well have given us bloody argument.
35   It might have since been answered in repaying
What we took from them; which, for traffic's sake,
Most of our city did; only myself stood out;
For which, if I be lapsed in this place,
I shall pay dear.

40 **Sebastian**   Do not then walk too open.

Antonio It doth not fit me. Hold, sir; here's my purse.
In the south suburbs, at the Elephant,
Is best to lodge; I will bespeak our diet,
Whiles you beguile the time and feed your knowledge
45   With viewing of the town; there shall you have me.

Sebastian Why I your purse?

Antonio Haply your eye shall light upon some toy
You have desire to purchase; and your store,
I think, is not for idle markets, sir.

50 **Sebastian** I'll be your purse-bearer, and leave you for an
hour.

Antonio To the Elephant.

Sebastian I do remember.

                                    [*Exeunt*]

Antonio   Please excuse me. I don't walk these streets without danger. Once, in a sea fight against Count Orsino's ships, I served so notably that if I were captured here it would be hard for me to defend my actions.

Sebastian   You killed many of his people?

Antonio   My offense was not so violent, although the circumstances of the occasion and the quarrel might well have given us cause for bloodshed. It might since have been dealt with by repaying what we took from them, which for the sake of trade, most people in our city did. I was the only one who refused. For which, if I'm caught in this place, I shall pay dearly.

Sebastian   Then don't walk about too openly.

Antonio   It doesn't suit me to hide. Wait, sir. Here's my purse. The Elephant inn in the south suburbs is the best place to stay. I will order our food while you pass the time and increase your knowledge by viewing the town. You'll find me at the inn.

Sebastian   Why should I have your purse?

Antonio   Perhaps you'll see some trifle you would like to buy, and the money you have will not, I think, permit luxuries.

Sebastian   I'll hold your purse and leave you for an hour.

Antonio   At the Elephant.

Sebastian   I'll remember.

[**Sebastian** *and* **Antonio** *exit in different directions*]

Act III

Scene IV

Olivia's Garden. Enter **Olivia** *and* **Maria.**

Olivia   I have sent after him; he says he'll come,
How shall I feast him? What bestow of him?
For youth is bought more oft than begged or borrowed.
I speak too loud.
5   Where is Malvolio? He is sad and civil,
And suits well for a servant with my fortunes;
Where is Malvolio?

Maria   He's coming, madam; but in very strange manner. He
is, sure, possessed, madam.

10 **Olivia**   Why, what's the matter? Does he rave?

Maria   No, madam; he does nothing but smile; your ladyship
were best to have some guard about you if he come, for
sure the man is tainted in's wits.

Olivia   Go call him hither.   [*Exit* **Maria**]
15 I am as mad as he,
If sad and merry madness equal be.

[*Enter* **Maria** *and* **Malvolio**]

How now, Malvolio!

Malvolio   Sweet lady, ho, ho.

Olivia's garden. **Olivia** *and* **Maria** *enter.*

Olivia [*to herself*] I have sent for him. Suppose he says he'll come. How shall I entertain him? What shall I give him? For youth is bought more often than begged or borrowed. [*She suddenly fears* **Maria** *can hear her*] I'm talking too loudly. [*To* **Maria**] Where is Malvolio? He is serious and proper, and as a servant suits well my current situation. Where is Malvolio?

Maria He's coming, madam, but acting in a very strange manner. He is surely out of his mind, madam.

Olivia Why, what's the matter? Is he raving?

Maria No, madam. He does nothing but smile. It would be best for your ladyship to have someone to guard you if he comes near. For surely the man's mind is unbalanced.

Olivia Go call him here. [**Maria** *leaves and returns with* **Malvolio**] I am as mad as he is, if to be sad and merry equals madness. How are you, Malvolio?

Malvolio Sweet lady! Ho, ho! [*smiling broadly and winking*]

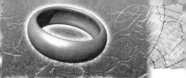

Olivia Smilest thou?
20   I sent for thee upon a sad occasion.

Malvolio Sad, lady! I could be sad; this does some obstruction
in the blood, this cross-gartering; but what of that? If it
please the eye of one, it is with me as the very true sonnet is,
'Please one, and please all'.

25 **Olivia** Why, how dost thou, man? What is the matter with
thee?

Malvolio Not black in my mind, though yellow in my legs. It
did come to his hands, and commands shall be executed; I
think we do know the sweet Roman hand.

30 **Olivia** Wilt thou go to bed, Malvolio?

Malvolio To bed! ay, sweetheart, and I'll come to thee.

Olivia God comfort thee! Why dost thou smile so, and kiss
thy hand so oft?

Maria How do you, Malvolio?

35 **Malvolio** At your request? Yes; nightingales answer daws.

Maria Why appear you with this ridiculous boldness before
my lady?

Malvolio 'Be not afraid of greatness'; 'twas well writ.

Olivia What meanest thou by that, Malvolio?

40 **Malvolio** 'Some are born great,' –

Olivia Ha!

Malvolio 'Some achieve greatness,' –

Olivia What sayest thou?

Malvolio 'And some have greatness thrust upon them.'

Olivia You smile? I sent for you about a sad matter.

Malvolio [*punning on* sad *meaning "serious"—Olivia's sense—and "unhappy"*] Sad, lady? I could be sad. This cross-gartering does restrict the blood supply, but what of it? If it pleases a certain eye, it is enough. As the poem very truly says, "Please one, please all."

Olivia Why, how are you, man? What is the matter with you?

Malvolio Not in a black humor—though yellow in my legs. It [*meaning Maria's letter*] did come into his hands, and its commands shall be carried out. I think we recognize the sweet Italian handwriting.

Olivia Shouldn't you go to bed, Malvolio?

Malvolio To bed? [*He blows several kisses at her and then quotes a popular song*] "Ay, sweetheart, and I'll come to thee."

Olivia God help you! Why do you smile like that, and kiss your hand so often?

Maria How are you, Malvolio?

Malvolio I must answer you? Do nightingales answer crows?

Maria Why do you act with this ridiculous boldness in front of my lady?

Malvolio "Do not be afraid of greatness." It was well written.

Olivia What do you mean by that, Malvolio?

Malvolio "Some are born great"—

Olivia What's that?

Malvolio "Some achieve greatness"—

Olivia What are you saying?

Malvolio "And some have greatness thrust upon them."

45 **Olivia** Heaven restore thee!

Malvolio 'Remember who commended thy yellow
      stockings,' –

Olivia Thy yellow stockings!

Malvolio 'And wished to see thee cross-gartered.'

50 **Olivia** Cross-gartered!

Malvolio 'Go to, thou art made, if thou desirest to be so;' –

Olivia Am I made?

Malvolio 'If not, let me see thee a servant still.'

Olivia Why, this is very midsummer madness.

      [*Enter* **Servant**]

55 **Servant** Madam, the young gentleman of the Count Orsino's
      is returned. I could hardly entreat him back; he attends
      your ladyship's pleasure.

Olivia I'll come to him.

                              [*Exit* **Servant**]

      Good Maria, let this fellow be looked to. Where's my cousin
60   Toby? Let some of my people have a special care of him; I
      would not have him miscarry for the half of my dowry.

                        [*Exeunt* **Olivia** *and* **Maria**]

Malvolio O, ho! do you come near me now? No worse man
      than Sir Toby to look to me! This concurs directly with the
      letter; she sends him on purpose that I may appear stubborn
65   to him; for she incites me to that in the letter, 'Cast thy
      humble slough,' says she; 'be opposite with a kinsman, surly
      with servants; let thy tongue tang with arguments of state; put

Olivia Heaven help you!

Malvolio "Remember who praised your yellow stockings"—

Olivia Your yellow stockings?

Malvolio "And wished to see you cross-gartered."

Olivia Cross-gartered?

Malvolio "Look here: you are certain of success if you want to be"—

Olivia I'm certain of success?

Malvolio "If not, stay a steward forever."

Olivia Why, this is truly midsummer madness!

[*A* **Servant** *enters*]

Servant Madam, Count Orsino's young gentleman has returned. It was hard to persuade him to come back. He awaits your ladyship's pleasure.

Olivia I'll come to him. [**Servant** *leaves*] Good Maria, let this fellow [*referring to* **Malvolio** *and used in the sense of "servant"*] be cared for. Where's my cousin Toby? Let some of my servants take special care of him. I would not have him come to harm for half of my fortune. [*She leaves with* **Maria**]

Malvolio Oh, ho! So you're beginning to understand me? No less important a person than Sir Toby to care for me! This agrees directly with the letter. She sends him on purpose, so that I may act rudely to him. For she encourages me to do that in the letter. "Cast off your humble manner," she said.

thyself into the trick of singularity'; and consequently sets
down the manner how; as, a sad face, a reverend carriage, a
70   slow tongue, in the habit of some air of note, and so forth. I
have limed her; but it is Jove's doing, and Jove make me
thankful! And when she went away now, 'Let this fellow be
looked to'; fellow! not Malvolio, nor after my degree, but
fellow. Why, everything adheres together, that no dram of a
75   scruple, no scruple of a scruple, no obstacle, no incredulous
or unsafe circumstance – What can be said? Nothing that
can be can come between me and the full prospect of my
hopes. Well, Jove, not I, is the doer of this, and he is to be
thanked.

[*Enter* **Maria,** *with* **Sir Toby Belch** *and* **Fabian**]

80   **Sir Toby** Which way is he, in the name of sanctity? If all the
devils of hell be drawn in little, and Legion himself
possessed him, yet I'll speak to him.

Fabian Here he is, here he is. How is't with you, sir?

Sir Toby How is't with you, man?

85   **Malvolio** Go off; I discard you; let me enjoy my private; go off.

Maria Lo, how hollow the fiend speaks within him! Did not
I tell you? Sir Toby, my lady prays you to have a care of him.

Malvolio Ah ha! does she so?

Sir Toby Go to, go to; peace! peace! We must deal gently
90   with him; let me alone. How do you, Malvolio? How is't
with you? What, man! defy the devil; consider, he's an
enemy to mankind.

Malvolio Do you know what you say?

"Be quarrelsome with a certain kinsman, and surly with the servants. Speak forthrightly about important matters; be eccentric." And following that, describes how it should be done: a serious face, a dignified walk, slow speech, in clothing suitable to some important gentleman, and so on. I've caught her, but it's heaven's doing, and heaven make me thankful! And to say as she went away just now, "Let this fellow be cared for." "Fellow!" [*He takes the word in the sense of "companion"*] Not "Malvolio." Not according to my place [*that is, steward*] but "fellow." Why, everything fits, so that no shadow of a doubt, no shadow of a shadow, no obstacle, no incredible or uncertain circumstance—What more can be said? Nothing can come between me and the fulfillment of my hopes. Well, heaven, not I, has done this, and heaven is to be thanked.

[**Sir Toby, Fabian,** *and* **Maria** *enter*]

Sir Toby Where is he, in the name of all that's holy? If all the devils in hell have been squeezed together and Satan himself possessed him, I'll still speak to him.

Fabian Here he is, here he is. How are you, sir?

Sir Toby How are you, man?

Malvolio Go away, I want nothing to do with you. Let me enjoy my privacy. Go away.

Maria Listen, how deep the devil speaks from inside him! Didn't I tell you? Sir Toby, my lady begs you to care for him.

Malvolio Ah ha! Does she indeed?

Sir Toby You don't say, you don't say! Hush, hush. We must deal gently with him. Leave him to me. How do you do, Malvolio? How are you? Come on, man, renounce the devil! Remember he's the enemy of mankind.

Malvolio Do you know what you're saying?

Maria La you! an you speak ill of the devil, how he takes it at
95 heart. Pray God, he be not bewitched!

Fabian Carry his water to the wise woman.

Maria Marry, and it shall be done tomorrow morning if I
live. My lady would not lose him for more than I'll say.

Malvolio How now, mistress!

100 **Maria** O Lord!

Sir Toby Prithee, hold thy peace; this is not the way; do you
not see you move him? Let me alone with him.

Fabian No way but gentleness; gently, gently; the fiend is
rough, and will not be roughly used.

105 **Sir Toby** Why, how now, my bawcock! how dost thou, chuck?

Malvolio Sir!

Sir Toby Ay, Biddy, come with me. What, man! 'tis not for
gravity to play at cherry-pit with Satan; hang him, foul
collier!

110 **Maria** Get him to say his prayers, good Sir Toby; get him to
pray.

Malvolio My prayers, minx!

Maria No, I warrant you, he will not hear of godliness.

Malvolio Go, hang yourselves all! You are idle, shallow
115 things; I am not of your element. You shall know more
hereafter.

[*Exit*]

Sir Toby Is't possible?

Maria [*to* **Sir Toby** *and* **Fabian**] Look, you two! When you speak ill of the devil, how he takes it to heart! Pray to God he isn't bewitched!

Fabian Let the healing woman examine him.

Maria Indeed, it shall be done tomorrow morning, I swear. My lady would not lose him for more than I can say.

Malvolio What's that, madam?

Maria Oh, Lord!

Sir Toby [*to* **Maria**] Please be quiet! This is not the way. Don't you see you're upsetting him? Leave me alone with him.

Fabian There's no way but gentleness. Gently, gently. The devil is rough and won't be treated roughly.

Sir Toby Why, how are you, my fine fellow? How are you doing, dear boy?

Malvolio [*offended*] Sir!

Sir Toby Yes, dearie, come with me. What, man, it's not dignified to play games with Satan. Hang him, he's filthy as a coal miner!

Maria Get him to say his prayers, good Sir Toby. Get him to pray.

Malvolio My prayers, impudent woman!

Maria No, I guarantee you, he will not hear of godliness.

Malvolio All of you go hang yourselves! You are foolish, worthless creatures. I am not on your level. You shall hear more about this later. [*He leaves*]

Sir Toby Is it possible?

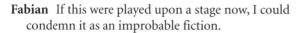

Fabian If this were played upon a stage now, I could condemn it as an improbable fiction.

120 **Sir Toby** His very genius hath taken the infection of the device, man.

Maria Nay, pursue him now, lest the device take air, and taint.

Fabian Why, we shall make him mad indeed.

125 **Maria** The house will be the quieter.

Sir Toby Come, we'll have him in a dark room, and bound. My niece is already in the belief that he's mad; we may carry it thus, for our pleasure and his penance, till our very pastime, tired out of breath, prompt us to have mercy on
130 him; at which time we will bring the device to the bar, and crown thee for a finder of madmen. But, see, but see.

[*Enter* **Sir Andrew Aguecheek**]

Fabian More matter for a May morning.

Sir Andrew Here's the challenge; read it; I warrant there's vinegar and pepper in't.

135 **Fabian** Is't so saucy?

Sir Andrew Ay, is't, I warrant him; do but read.

Sir Toby Give me. [*Reading*] 'Youth, whatsoever thou art, thou art but a scurvy fellow.'

Fabian Good and valiant.

140 **Sir Toby** 'Wonder not, nor admire not in thy mind, why I do call thee so, for I will show thee no reason for't.'

Fabian A good note, that keeps you from the blow of the law.

Fabian If this were being acted on the stage now, I would condemn it as a highly unlikely story.

Sir Toby He has fallen heart and soul for the trick, man.

Maria But you must keep after him, before he gets wise to the trick.

Fabian Why, we shall make him *really* mad.

Maria The house will be quieter without him.

Sir Toby [*describing the common treatment for insanity*] Come on, we'll have him tied up and put in a dark room. My niece has already begun to believe he's mad. In this way, we can keep it up—for our amusement and his punishment—until we're so tired and out of breath with our pastime that we're prompted to have mercy on him. At that point we'll confess the trick and [*to* **Maria**] crown you as a finder of madmen. [*He sees* **Sir Andrew** *coming*] But see who's here!

[**Sir Andrew** *enters*]

Fabian More material for a May-day farce.

Sir Andrew Here's the challenge. Read it. I guarantee there's vinegar and pepper in it.

Fabian Is it so saucy?

Sir Andrew Yes it is. I guarantee it. But do read.

Sir Toby Give it to me. [*Reads*] "Youth, whoever you are, you are nothing but a contemptible fellow."

Fabian Good and bold.

Sir Toby [*reads*] "Do not be amazed, nor marvel in your mind, why I call you that. Because I will give you no reason for it."

Fabian A good point; that keeps you safe from the law.

Sir Toby 'Thou comest to the Lady Olivia, and in my sight
she uses thee kindly; but thou liest in thy throat, and that is
145 not the matter I challenge thee for.'

Fabian Very brief, and to exceeding good sense-less.

Sir Toby 'I will waylay thee going home; where, if it be thy
chance to kill me, –'

Fabian Good.

150 **Sir Toby** 'Thou killest me like a rogue and a villain.'

Fabian Still you keep o' the windy side of the law; good.

Sir Toby 'Fare thee well; and God have mercy upon one of
our souls! He may have mercy upon mine, but my hope is
better; and so look to thyself. Thy friend, as thou usest him,
155 and thy sworn enemy,

                                   Andrew Aguecheek'

If this letter move him not, his legs cannot. I'll give't him.

Maria You may have very fit occasion for't; he is now in some
commerce with my lady, and will by and by depart.

160 **Sir Toby** Go, Sir Andrew; scout me for him at the corner of
the orchard, like a bum-baily; so soon as ever thou seest him,
draw; and, as thou drawest, swear horrible; for it comes to
pass oft that a terrible oath, with a swaggering accent sharply
twanged off, gives manhood more approbation than ever
165 proof itself would have earned him. Away!

Sir Andrew Nay, let me alone for swearing.

                                        [*Exit*]

Sir Toby Now will not I deliver his letter; for the behaviour
of the young gentleman gives him out to be of good capacity
and breeding; his employment between his lord and my niece
170 confirms no less; therefore this letter, being so excellently
ignorant, will breed no terror in the youth; he will find it

Sir Toby [*reads*] "You come to see the Lady Olivia, and right in front of me she treats you well. But you're lying in your teeth. That's not the reason I'm challenging you."

Fabian Very brief, and quite sense- [*to himself*] less.

Sir Toby [*reads*] "I will waylay you as you go home, and if by chance you kill me—"

Fabian Good.

Sir Toby [*reads*] "—you would kill me like a rogue and a villain."

Fabian You're still on the safe side of the law; good.

Sir Toby [*reads*] "Farewell, and God have mercy on one of our souls! He may have mercy on mine. But my hope of surviving is better, so protect yourself! Your friend—if you treat him so—and your sworn enemy,

Sir Andrew Aguecheek."

If this letter doesn't stir him, then his legs can't. I'll give it to him.

Maria You may have a very convenient opportunity to do so; he is now conversing with my lady and seems about to leave.

Sir Toby Go, Sir Andrew, and keep watch for him at a corner of the garden like a sheriff's deputy. As soon as you see him, draw your sword, and as you draw it, swear horribly. For it often happens that a terrible oath, spoken in a swaggering voice, gives a man a greater reputation for valor than actual performance would have earned him. Away!

Sir Andrew Leave the swearing to me! [*He leaves*]

Sir Toby [*to* **Fabian**] Now, I won't deliver this letter, because the behavior of the young gentleman indicates him to be a capable and well-bred person. His employment as a messenger between his lord and my niece equally confirms this. Therefore this letter, being so completely idiotic, will inspire no terror in the youth; he will see it comes from a knucklehead. Instead, sir, I will deliver

comes from a clodpole. But, sir, I will deliver his challenge
by word of mouth; set upon Aguecheek a notable report of
valour; and drive the gentleman, as I know his youth will
175   aptly receive it, into a most hideous opinion of his rage, skill,
fury, and impetuosity. This will so fright them both that
they will kill one another by the look, like cockatrices.

Fabian Here he comes with your niece; give them way till he
take leave, and presently after him.

180 **Sir Toby** I will meditate the while upon some horrid message for a challenge.

[*Exeunt* **Sir Toby, Fabian** *and* **Maria**]

[*Enter* **Olivia** *and* **Viola**]

Olivia I have said too much unto a heart of stone,
And laid mine honour too unchary on't;
There's something in me that reproves my fault,
185   But such a headstrong potent fault it is
That it but mocks reproof.

Viola With the same 'haviour that your passion bears,
Goes on my master's grief.

Olivia Here; wear this jewel for me; 'tis my picture;
190   Refuse it not; it hath no tongue to vex you;
And I beseech you come again tomorrow.
What shall you ask of me that I'll deny,
That honour saved may upon asking give?

Viola Nothing but this: your true love for my master.

195 **Olivia** How with mine honour may I give him that
Which I have given to you?

his challenge by word of mouth. I will give Aguecheek an outstanding reputation for valor, and give the young gentleman—who being so inexperienced, will easily accept it—a shocking belief of his rage, skill, fury, and rashness. They will both be so frightened that they will kill one another with mere looks, like mythical cockatrices were believed to do.

Fabian   Here he comes with your niece. Stay out of their way until he leaves, and immediately follow him.

Sir Toby   Meanwhile, I will think about some terrifying message for the challenge.

[**Sir Toby, Fabian,** *and* **Maria** *exit*]

[**Olivia** *and* **Viola** *enter*]

Olivia   I have said too much to a heart of stone, and carelessly risked my honor. There is something inside me that disapproves of my fault; but it's such a stubborn, powerful fault that it simply scorns disapproval.

Viola   My master's grief behaves the same way as your passion.

Olivia   Here, wear this locket for me. It has my picture. Don't refuse; it has no tongue to annoy you. And I beg you to come again tomorrow. What could you ask of me that I would deny if I could give it honorably?

Viola   Nothing but this—your true love for my master.

Olivia   How can I honorably give him that which I have given you?

Viola   I will acquit you.

Olivia Well, come again tomorrow; fare you well;
A fiend like thee might bear my soul to hell.

[*Exit*]

[*Enter* **Sir Toby Belch** *and* **Fabian**]

200   **Sir Toby** Gentleman, God save thee.

Viola And you, sir.

Sir Toby That defence thou hast, betake thee to't; of what
nature the wrongs are thou hast done him, I know not; but
thy intercepter, full of despite, bloody as the hunter, attends
205   thee at the orchard-end. Dismount thy tuck, be yare in thy
preparation, for thy assailant is quick, skilful, and deadly.

Viola You mistake, sir; I am sure no man hath any quarrel to
me; my remembrance is very free and clear from any image
of offence done to any man.

210   **Sir Toby** You'll find it otherwise, I assure you; therefore, if
you hold your life at any price, betake you to your guard; for
your opposite hath in him what youth, strength, skill, and
wrath can furnish man withal.

Viola I pray you sir, what is he?

215   **Sir Toby** He is knight, dubbed with unhatched rapier, and
on carpet consideration; but he is a devil in a private brawl;
souls and bodies hath he divorced three, and his incensement
at this moment is so implacable that satisfaction can be none
but by pangs of death and sepulchre. Hob, nob, is his word;
220   give't or take't.

Viola I will return again into the house, and desire some
conduct of the lady: I am no fighter. I have heard of some

Viola I release you from your promise.

Olivia Well, come again tomorrow. Farewell. A devil that looked like you could take my soul to hell.

[**Olivia** *exits*]

[**Sir Toby** *and* **Fabian** *enter*]

Sir Toby Gentleman, God save you!

Viola And you, sir.

Sir Toby Whatever skill in fencing you have, apply yourself to it. I don't know what kind of wrongs you've done him, but your adversary—filled with hatred and out for blood—waits for you at the end of the garden. Draw your sword, and stand ready, for your attacker is quick, skillful, and deadly.

Viola You must be mistaken, sir, I'm sure. No man has any quarrel with me. My memory is completely free and clear of a recollection of a wrong done to any man.

Sir Toby You'll find it otherwise, I assure you. Therefore, if you value your life at all, apply yourself to your defense. For your adversary has everything that youth, strength, skill, and wrath can give him.

Viola I beg you, sir, who is he?

Sir Toby He is a knight, although dubbed with an ornamental sword at court, and not for battlefield service, but he is a devil in private brawls. He has killed three men, and he is so enraged at this moment that there is no satisfying him except with mortal wounds and the grave. "Have or have not" is his motto; kill or be killed.

Viola I will return to the house, and ask the lady for an escort. I am no fighter. I have heard that some men pick quarrels with

kind of men that put quarrels purposely on others to taste
their valour; belike this is a man of that quirk.

225 **Sir Toby** Sir, no; his indignation derives itself out of a very
competent injury! Therefore get you on and give him his
desire. Back you shall not to the house, unless you undertake that with me which with as much safety you might
answer him; therefore on, or strip your sword stark naked;
230 for meddle you must, that's certain, or forswear to wear
iron about you.

Viola This is as uncivil as strange. I beseech you, do me this
courteous office, as to know of the knight what my offence
to him is; it is something of my negligence, nothing of my
235 purpose.

Sir Toby I will do so. Signior Fabian, stay you by this
gentleman till my return.

[*Exit*]

Viola Pray you, sir, do you know of this matter?

Fabian I know the knight is incensed against you, even to a
240 mortal arbitrement, but nothing of the circumstance more.

Viola I beseech you, what manner of man is he?

Fabian Nothing of that wonderful promise, to read him by
his form, as you are like to find him in the proof of his
valour. He is indeed, sir, the most skilful, bloody, and fatal
245 opposite that you could possibly have found in any part of
Illyria. Will you walk towards him? I will make your peace
with him if I can.

Viola I shall be much bound to you for't; I am one that had
rather go with sir priest than sir knight; I care not who
250 knows so much of my mettle.

[*Exeunt*]

others, to test their valor. Probably this is a man with that odd trait.

Sir Toby No, sir; his anger results from a very real injury. Therefore you better go on, and give him satisfaction. You shall not go back to the house, unless you're willing to fight me, which would be as risky as facing him. Therefore, go on, or draw your sword now and fight me. For duel you must, or give up wearing a sword.

Viola This is as rude as it is strange. I beg you to do me this courteous service: ask the knight how I offended him. It must be something I neglected, not something I intended.

Sir Toby I will do so. Mister Fabian, you stay with this gentleman till my return.

[**Sir Toby** *exits*]

Viola Please, sir, do you know of this matter?

Fabian I know the knight is so angry with you that it requires a duel to the death. But I don't know anything more of the circumstances.

Viola I beg you, what kind of man is he?

Fabian To judge by his appearance, there is no extraordinary indication of what you are likely to discover about him when you test his valor. He is indeed, sir, the most skillful, violent, and deadly opponent that you could possibly have found in any part of Illyria. If you will walk toward him, I will make peace between you and him if I can.

Viola I will be very obliged to you for it. I am a person that would much rather go with Sir priest than Sir knight. And I don't care who knows that about my character.

[**Viola** *and* **Fabian** *exit*]

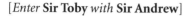

[*Enter* **Sir Toby** *with* **Sir Andrew**]

Sir Toby Why, man, he's a very devil; I have not seen such a firago. I had a pass with him, rapier, scabbard, and all, and he gives me the tuck-in with such a mortal motion that it is inevitable; and on the answer, he pays you as surely as your
255 feet hit the ground they step on. They say he has been fencer to the Sophy.

Sir Andrew Pox on't, I'll not meddle with him.

Sir Toby Ay, but he will not now be pacified; Fabian can scarce hold him yonder.

260 **Sir Andrew** Plague on't; an I thought he had been valiant and so cunning in fence I'd have seen him damned ere I'd have challenged him. Let him let the matter slip, and I'll give him my horse, grey Capilet.

Sir Toby I'll make the motion. Stand here; make a good show
265 on't; this shall end without the perdition of souls. [*Aside*] Marry, I'll ride your horse as well as I ride you.

[*Enter* **Fabian** *and* **Viola**]

I have his horse to take up the quarrel. I have persuaded him, the youth's a devil.

Fabian He is as horribly conceited of him; and pants and
270 looks pale, as if a bear were at his heels.

Sir Toby There's no remedy, sir; he will fight with you for's oath sake. Marry, he hath better bethought him of his quarrel, and he finds that now scarce to be worth talking of; therefore draw for the supportance of his vow; he protests he
275 will not hurt you.

Viola Pray God defend me! A little thing would make me tell them how much I lack of a man.

[**Sir Toby** *and* **Sir Andrew** *enter*]

Sir Toby Why man, he's a true devil. I've never seen such a firebrand. I had an exchange with him—sword, sheath, and all, and he gave me a thrust with such a deadly accuracy that it was unavoidable. And my return thrust he parried as surely as you're standing there. They say he has been a fencer for the shah of Persia.

Sir Andrew Plague take it! I'll not duel with him.

Sir Toby Yes, but he won't be pacified now. Fabian can scarcely hold him back.

Sir Andrew Plague take it! If I knew he was so valiant, and such a skillful fencer, I would have seen him damned before I'd have challenged him. If he'll let the matter go, I'll give him my horse, gray Capilet.

Sir Toby I'll make the offer. Stand here, and act tough. This will end without loss of life. [*To himself*] Indeed, I'll ride your horse as well as I ride you.

[**Fabian** *and* **Viola** *enter*]

[*To* **Fabian**] I have his horse to settle the quarrel. I have persuaded him the youth's a devil.

Fabian The youth is equally frightened of him. He gasps and looks pale as if a bear were after him.

Sir Toby [*to* **Viola**] There's no remedy, sir. He will fight with you for the sake of his honor. Indeed, he's had second thoughts about the reason for the duel, and now thinks that it's scarcely worth talking about. Therefore, draw your sword, to keep his vow. He promises he won't hurt you.

Viola [*to herself*] Pray God defend me! It would take little more for me to tell them that I am not a man.

Fabian Give ground, if you see him furious.

Sir Toby Come, Sir Andrew, there's no remedy; the
280 gentleman will, for his honour's sake, have one bout with
you; he cannot by the duello avoid it; but he has promised me,
as he is a gentleman and a soldier, he will not hurt you.
Come on; to't.

Sir Andrew Pray God, he keeps his oath! [*Draws his sword*]

285 **Viola** I do assure you, 'tis against my will. [*Draws his sword*]

    [*Enter* **Antonio**]

Antonio Put up your sword. If this young gentleman
Have done offence, I take the fault on me;
If you offend him, I for him defy you. [*Draws his sword*]

Sir Toby You sir! Why, what are you?

290 **Antonio** One, sir, that for his love dares yet do more
Than you have heard him brag to you he will.

Sir Toby Nay, if you be an undertaker, I am for you. [*Draws
his sword*]

Fabian O good Sir Toby, hold! Here come the officers.

    [*Enter* **Officers**]

Sir Toby I'll be with you anon.

295 **Viola** Pray, sir, put your sword up, if you please.

Sir Andrew Marry, will I, sir; and, for that I promised you,
I'll be as good as my word. He will bear you easily, and reins
well.

1st Officer This is the man; do thy office.

Fabian [*to* **Viola**] Retreat if you see him furious.

Sir Toby Come, Sir Andrew, there's no remedy. The gentleman will have one bout with you for his honor's sake. By the code of dueling, he can't avoid it. But he has promised me, as he is a gentleman and a soldier, that he will not hurt you. Come on, go to it!

Sir Andrew Pray God he keep his oath! [*He draws his sword*]

Viola [*to* **Sir Andrew**] I do assure you, it's against my will. [*She draws her sword*]

[**Antonio** *enters*]

Antonio [*to* **Sir Andrew**] Put up your sword. If this young gentleman has offended you, I will answer for it. If you have offended him, I challenge you on his behalf. [*He draws his sword*]

Sir Toby You, sir! Why, who are you?

Antonio One, sir, that for love of this young man will dare to do even more than he has bragged to you that he will.

Sir Toby Well, if you're taking up his challenge, then I'm ready for you! [*He draws his sword*]

Fabian Oh good Sir Toby, stop! Here come the officers.

[*Two* **Officers** *enter*]

Sir Toby [*to* **Antonio**] I'll attend to you shortly.

Viola [*to* **Sir Andrew**] Please sir, put your sword away, if you would.

Sir Andrew Indeed I will, sir. And about that which I promised you, [*meaning his horse*] I'll be as good as my word. He will carry you smoothly and is easy to manage.

1st Officer [*indicating* **Antonio**] This is the man. Do your duty.

300 **2nd Officer** Antonio, I arrest thee at the suit
Of Count Orsino.

Antonio   You do mistake me, sir.

1st Officer No, sir, no jot; I know your favour well,
Though now you have no sea-cap on your head.
305 Take him away; he knows I know him well.

Antonio I must obey. [*To* **Viola**] This comes with seeking you;
But there's no remedy; I shall answer it.
What will you do, now my necessity
Makes me to ask you for my purse? It grieves me
310 Much more for what I cannot do for you
Than what befalls myself. You stand amazed;
But be of comfort.

2nd Officer Come, sir, away.

Antonio I must entreat of you some of that money.

315 **Viola** What money, sir?
For the fair kindness you have showed me here,
And part, being prompted by your present trouble,
Out of my lean and low ability
I'll lend you something; my having is not much;
320 I'll make division of my present with you.
Hold, here is half my coffer.

Antonio   Will you deny me now?
Is't possible that my deserts to you
Can lack persuasion? Do not tempt my misery,
325 Lest that it make me so unsound a man
As to upbraid you with those kindnesses
That I have done for you.

Viola   I know of none;
Nor know I you by voice or any feature.
330 I hate ingratitude more in a man
Than lying, vainness, babbling drunkenness,
Or any taint of vice whose strong corruption
Inhabits our frail blood.

2nd Officer [*to* **Antonio**] I arrest you on the order of Count Orsino.

Antonio You're mistaking me for someone else, sir.

1st Officer No, sir; not a bit. I know your face well, though now you have no seaman's cap on your head. [*To* **2nd Officer**] Take him away. He knows I know him well.

Antonio I will obey. [*To* **Viola**] This comes from seeking you. But there's no remedy. I shall have to face it. What will you do, now that my need forces me to ask you to return my purse? I am far more unhappy about my inability to help you than about what happens to me. You stand there bewildered. Cheer up.

2nd Officer Come on, sir; let's go.

Antonio [*to* **Viola**] I must beg of you some of that money.

Viola What money, sir? In return for the generous kindness you have shown me here, and partly in response to your present trouble, I'll lend you something from my slender and small means. I don't have much. I'll split my ready money with you. Look, here's half my wealth.

Antonio Will you deny me now? Is it possible that my services to you can fail to persuade you? Don't try me too far in my misery, lest it make me forget myself. Then I might blame you because of those kindnesses that I have done for you.

Viola I don't know of any. Nor do I know you by your voice or any feature. I hate ingratitude in a man more than lying, vanity, babbling drunkenness, or any of the other faults that badly corrupt our frail human natures.

Antonio   O heavens themselves!

335   **2nd Officer**   Come, sir, I pray you, go.

     Antonio   Let me speak a little. This youth that you see here
         I snatched one-half out of the jaws of death,
         Relieved him with such sanctity of love,
         And to his image, which methought did promise
340   Most venerable worth, did I devotion.

     1st Officer   What's that to us? The time goes by; away!

     Antonio   But O! how vile an idol proves this god!
         Thou hast, Sebastian, done good feature shame.
         In nature there's no blemish but the mind;
345   None can be called deformed but the unkind;
         Virtue is beauty, but the beauteous evil
         Are empty trunks o'erflourished by the devil.

     1st Officer   The man grows mad; away with him! Come,
     come, sir.

350   **Antonio**   Lead me on.

                    [*Exeunt* **Officers** *with* **Antonio**]

     Viola   Methinks his words do from such passion fly,
         That he believes himself; so do not I.
         Prove true, imagination. O! prove true,
         That I, dear brother, be now ta'en for you.

355   **Sir Toby**   Come hither, knight; come hither, Fabian; we'll
     whisper o'er a couplet or two of most sage saws.

     Viola   He named Sebastian; I my brother know
         Yet living in my glass; even such and so
         In favour was my brother; and he went
360   Still in his fashion, colour, ornament,
         For him I imitate. O! if it prove,
         Tempests are kind, and salt waves fresh in love.

                             [*Exit*]

Antonio Oh good heavens!

2nd Officer Come on, sir; please go.

Antonio Let me speak a little more. This youth that you see here, I rescued when he was half-drowned. I cared for him with a great, loving devotion, and worshipped what he appeared to be, which seemed worthy of reverence.

1st Officer What's that to us? We're wasting time. Let's go!

Antonio But oh, how wretched an idol this god proves to be! Sebastian, you have brought shame on beauty. In nature, there is no real defect but in the mind. Only the unkind can be called deformed. Virtue is beauty, but those who are beautiful but evil inside are empty boxes ornamented by the devil.

1st Officer [*to* **2nd Officer**] The man's mad. Take him away! [*To* **Antonio**] Come on, sir, come on.

Antonio Take me away. [*He leaves with* **Officers**]

Viola [*to herself*] He speaks so passionately that I think he believes what he says. I wish I could! Prove to be true, imagination. Oh, prove to be true! That I, dear brother, am now mistaken for you!

Sir Toby [*to* **Sir Andrew** *and* **Fabian**] Come here, knight. Come here, Fabian. Let's share a few wise words.

Viola [*to herself*] He called me Sebastian. I still see my brother alive when I look in the mirror. My brother's face looked just like this, and this. [*She indicates different facial features*] And he always wore clothes of this color and style, [*indicating her clothing*] and I've imitated him. Oh, if it proves true, storms are friendly, and salt waves full of love.

Personification

[**Viola** *exits*]

Sir Toby A very dishonest paltry boy, and more a coward
than a hare. His dishonesty appears in leaving his friend here
365   in necessity, and denying him; and for his cowardship, ask
Fabian.

Fabian A coward, a most devout coward, religious in it.

Sir Andrew 'Slid, I'll after him again, and beat him.

Sir Toby Do; cuff him soundly, but never draw thy sword.

370 **Sir Andrew** An I do not, –

                                                      [*Exit*]

Fabian Come, let's see the event.

Sir Toby I dare lay any money 'twill be nothing yet.

                                                   [*Exeunt*]

Sir Toby A very dishonorable, contemptible boy, and more cowardly than a rabbit. He shows his dishonorableness by abandoning his friend here in need, and denying he knew him. And as for his cowardice, ask Fabian.

Fabian A coward, a most devout coward, quite religious about it.

Sir Andrew By God, I'll follow him and beat him.

Sir Toby Do that; beat him soundly. But don't draw your sword.

Sir Andrew If I do not— [*The rest of his threat is lost as he exits*]

Fabian Come on, let's see what happens.

Sir Toby I'll bet any money it will be nothing.

[**Sir Toby** *and* **Fabian** *exit*]

Comprehension Check What You Know

1. When Viola/Cesario visits Olivia, why does Sir Andrew point out some of the words that Viola/Cesario uses to greet her?

2. What does Viola/Cesario return to Olivia? Why does Olivia apologize?

3. Olivia admits how much she loves Cesario, and Viola/Cesario says, "I pity you." Why does that encourage Olivia? What other things encourage her, even though Viola/Cesario is trying to discourage her?

4. Sir Andrew says that he is going to leave. Why? How do Sir Toby and Fabian talk him out of going? Why does Sir Toby want Sir Andrew to stay?

5. What do Sir Toby and Fabian talk Sir Andrew into doing? How do they say this will appeal to Olivia?

6. What does Maria tell Fabian and Sir Toby?

7. Why has Antonio followed Sebastian to the city? Why don't they tour the city together? When they separate, where do they go?

8. How does Malvolio act when he comes to see Olivia? What does she think is wrong with him? What does she tell Maria?

9. Sir Toby, Fabian, and Maria all act as if they don't know what has led Malvolio to act as he does. What do they decide is the best thing to do?

10. Does Sir Toby deliver Sir Andrew's letter to Viola/Cesario? Why?

11. How do Viola/Cesario and Sir Andrew try to get out of the duel? What "bribes" do they propose?

12. Who saves Viola/Cesario? Why does he do that? Who does he think Viola/Cesario is? What happens to Antonio?

Melissa Bowen as Olivia and Floyd King as Malvolio in The Shakespeare Theater's 1998 production of *Twelfth Night* directed by Daniel Fish. Photo by Carol Rosegg.

Activities & Role-Playing **Classes or Book Clubs**

What Did You Say? Working with three others, read through the scene of the confrontation between Malvolio and Olivia (Scene 4, lines 18–54) and discuss their attitudes, emotions, and interactions. Then discuss the *irony* in the scene. Remember, both characters are operating from different ideas about what is going on. Malvolio believes he is behaving the way that Olivia wants him to—that she loves him and wants him to marry her. Olivia, of course, is totally ignorant of his beliefs—and they are the farthest things from her mind!

My Sword, My Sword! Why does Sir Toby want Sir Andrew and Cesario to have a duel? Does he want to see someone injured? Does he want to see each man make a fool of himself? Or is there some other reason? Be sure to use lines from the play to prove your points.

Discussion **Classes or Book Clubs**

1. Maria has gulled Malvolio. Talk about the way that Sir Toby gulls Sir Andrew. What characteristics of Sir Andrew does Toby take advantage of? Why is Sir Andrew fair game for gulling?

2. Fabian is a minor character and has to be included for a reason. What does this minor character add to this scene?

3. Olivia is sure that Cesario is beginning to love her. After all, he pities her. Sir Toby and Fabian use Sir Andrew's ideas about romantic love to talk him into the duel with Cesario. Both Olivia and Sir Andrew are objects of humor because of their ideas about love. Discuss those ideas. Then discuss the play's ideas about a healthier, more realistic kind of love.

4. A good example of irony is in Scene 4, lines 137–157, when Fabian and Sir Toby read Sir Andrew's letter to Cesario. The irony begins immediately. When Sir Andrew enters the room, Fabian says, "Here's more matter for a May day." In other words, here's someone else ripe for gulling. Read this section, and discuss what Fabian and Toby say—and what they mean—as they praise Sir Andrew's letter. Then find other examples of irony in Scene 4.

Suggestions for Writing **Improve Your Skills**

1. By now you know quite a bit about Viola's personality. Pretend that you're writing a letter to a friend and want to describe this woman's very unusual situation. Explain what you like about her—and what you don't.

2. Olivia is sure that Cesario is the one for her. Write a diary entry that describes her feelings for him. Then compare them with the feelings you had about your first love.

All the World's a Stage Introduction

The world of Illyria becomes curiouser and curiouser. Viola/Cesario has tried one more time to court Olivia for the Duke and again found that it is impossible to discuss it with her because she has given her heart to Cesario. Malvolio has donned yellow, cross-gartered stockings and has been roundly rejected by Olivia, who is certain that her steward has gone mad. Sir Toby has talked Sir Andrew into dueling with Cesario (Olivia will be won over by any wounds that Sir Andrew receives, assures Toby). He also has convinced Cesario that he must take part in the duel, even though Cesario insists he isn't any good at swordfighting. And Antonio, mistaking Cesario for Sebastian, has been hauled off to prison after coming to Cesario's rescue and now believes that Sebastian has proven to be a poor friend for rejecting him for no good reason. The only person who remains outside the wild events is Sebastian, and you *know* that he can't avoid it much longer.

What's in a Name? Characters

Everyone is now in a stew, and it's partly because in Illyria falling in love at a moment's notice is not unusual—it's the norm! Orsino says that he fell in love with Olivia when he saw her for the very first time. Olivia says that she has been stricken with love for Cesario as if she had caught the plague. Viola never explains when or why she fell in love with the Duke; she just says that it has happened. And Sir Toby says that he should marry Maria because her gulling of Malvolio is so cleverly done. How can all this be normal? Viola perhaps had the key when she said that Fate would have to work things out because she certainly can't figure it out. When things happen so randomly, it may seem that larger forces are at work.

COME WHAT MAY Things to Watch For

Viola is pretending to be something that she is not—a man. But she's not the only one pretending. It seems like Olivia was pretending her grief when she throws it over so quickly when she meets Cesario. Malvolio pretended to be the merry lover, which is completely out of character for him. Maria pretended to be confused and concerned over Malvolio's behavior and agreed to have Sir Toby come and "take care of" the mad steward.

In Act 4 two other people will become pretenders. One of them, to play his role successfully, must wear an appropriate costume. The second person becomes a pretender when he is mistaken for someone who is dearly loved—and goes along with the confusion, simply because he is completely enchanted and has himself fallen in love immediately.

All Our Yesterdays Historical and Social Context

One question that arises when you hear about Malvolio's aspirations to marry Olivia is this: How realistic is his goal?

The social order was changing in Shakespeare's time. Trading companies were growing, as were mining and manufacturing. Prosperity, at least for some people, was growing. Landowners and other influential families were becoming more important at the English court. It was also possible to marry into a wealthy family. In fact, William Ffarington, a steward to an English lord, disinherited his son when he refused to marry a wealthy woman from a family that was higher on the social ladder! (Malvolio would have liked Mr. Ffarington.)

Still, most people would have been as upset as Sir Toby at Malvolio's ambitions. When Toby hears Malvolio describing how he would treat him, Toby almost spoils the trick by jumping out and bopping Malvolio over the head!

Another way to judge Malvolio's ambition is to compare him with Olivia. One of the first questions she asks Cesario is about his family status. He says that he is a gentleman—that tells her that he's from a noble family. Only then does she express her interest in him.

The Play's the Thing Staging

Playgoing had a long tradition in England. Most commentators believe Shakespeare had seen *morality plays*. In them, actors represent a characteristic instead of a person. Roles in morality plays would be Honor, Patience, or Greed. Vice, a comic character, was an early version of the traditional fool. In Act 4, Feste compares himself with Vice when he sings that he will return "Like to the old Vice" with "his dagger of lath" and "his rage and his wrath." This is a reference to the morality plays in which Vice would beat the Devil with his wooden dagger, then threaten to trim the Devil's nails with it. According to the joke, of course, it is the Devil inside Malvolio that has made him crazy.

My Words Fly Up Language

In Act 4, the joke on Malvolio continues. Feste puts on a disguise to become Sir Topas, a clergyman come to question the steward and see if he is still mad or if his environment has cured him. The name is another joke, because at this time people believed that wearing a topaz, a semi-precious stone, would cure madness.

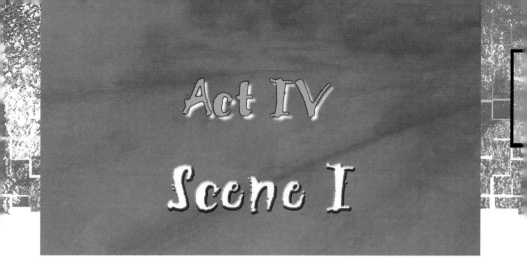

Act IV

Scene I

Before Olivia's House. Enter **Sebastian** *and* **Feste.**

Feste Will you make me believe that I am not sent for you?

Sebastian Go to, go to; thou are a foolish fellow;
Let me be clear of thee.

Feste Well held out, i'faith! No, I do not know you; nor I am
5   not sent to you by my lady to bid you come speak with her;
nor your name is not Master Cesario; nor this is not my nose
neither. Nothing that is so is so.

Sebastian I prithee, vent thy folly somewhere else;
Thou know'st not me.

10 **Feste** Vent my folly! He has heard that word of some great
man, and now applies it to a fool. Vent my folly! I am afraid
this great lubber, the world, will prove a cockney. I prithee
now, ungird thy strangeness and tell me what I shall vent to
my lady. Shall I vent to her that thou art coming?

15 **Sebastian** I prithee, foolish Greek, depart from me;
There's money for thee; if you tarry longer
I shall give worse payment.

Feste By my troth, thou hast an open hand. These wise men
that give fools money get themselves a good report – after
20   fourteen years' purchase.

[*Enter* **Sir Andrew**]

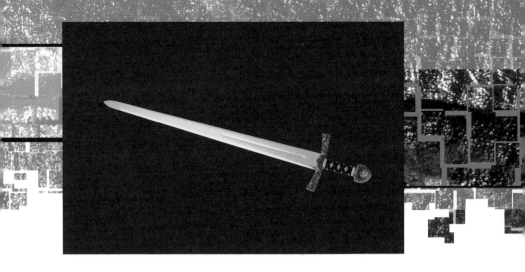

In front of Olivia's house. **Sebastian** and **Feste** enter.

Feste   Are you trying to make me believe I wasn't sent for you?

Sebastian   Enough, enough! You are a foolish fellow. Let me be rid of you.

Feste   You're keeping up this act very well indeed! No, I don't know you. Nor was I sent to you by my lady, to ask you to come speak with her. Nor is your name Master Cesario. Nor is this my nose, either. Nothing that is so, is so.

Sebastian   Please give vent to your folly somewhere else. You don't know me.

Feste   [*to himself*] "Vent" to my folly! He's heard that word used by some important man and now applies it to a fool. Vent to my folly! I am afraid that this great lout of a world is becoming a fop. [*To* **Sebastian**] Please stop pretending not to know me and tell me what I shall "vent" to my lady. Shall I "vent" to her that you are coming?

Sebastian   Please, foolish jester, leave me. Here's money for you. If you stay any longer, I'll give you worse payment.

Feste   By my faith, you're generous. These wise men that give fools money get themselves a good reputation—at an inflated price!

   [**Sir Andrew** *enters*]

Sir Andrew Now, sir, have I met you again? There's for you.

[*Striking* **Sebastian**]

Sebastian Why, there's for thee, and there, and there.
[*Beating* **Sir Andrew**] Are all the people mad?

[*Enter* **Sir Toby** *and* **Fabian**]

Sir Toby Hold, sir, or I'll throw your dagger o'er the house.

[*They seize* **Sebastian**]

25 **Feste** This will I tell my lady straight. I would not be in some of
your coats for twopence.

[*Exeunt*]

Sir Toby Come on, sir; hold.

Sir Andrew Nay, let him alone; I'll go another way to work
with him; I'll have an action of battery against him if there be
30 any law in Illyria. Though I struck him first, yet it's no
matter for that.

Sebastian Let go thy hand.

Sir Toby Come, sir, I will not let you go. Come, my young
soldier, put up your iron; you are well fleshed; come on.

35 **Sebastian** I will free from thee. What would'st thou now?
If thou dar'st tempt me further, draw thy sword.

Sir Toby What, what! Nay, then I must have an ounce or
two of this malapert blood from you.

[*Enter* **Olivia**]

Sir Andrew [*to* **Sebastian,** *mistaking him for* **Viola**] Now, sir, we meet again! Here's something for you! [*He strikes* **Sebastian**]

Sebastian Why, here's something for you! [*He strikes* **Sir Andrew** *with the handle of his dagger*] And this! And this! [*He strikes him twice more*] Are all these people insane?

[**Sir Toby** *and* **Fabian** *enter*]

Sir Toby [*to* **Sebastian,** *seizing his arm*] Stop that, sir, or I'll throw your dagger over the house.

Feste I'll report this to my lady immediately. [*To* **Sir Toby**] I wouldn't be in your shoes for money.

[**Feste** *exits*]

Sir Toby [*to* **Sebastian**] Come on, sir. Stop it!

Sir Andrew No, let him alone. I'll get at him in another way. I'll sue him for assault, if there's any law in Illyria. Though I struck him first, that doesn't matter.

Sebastian [*to* **Sir Toby**] Take your hand off me!

Sir Toby Come on, sir, I will not let you go. Come on, my young soldier, put away your dagger. You've drawn first blood. [*He refers to* **Sebastian** *striking* **Sir Andrew** *with his dagger*] Come on.

Sebastian I will be free of you. [*He breaks free and draws his sword*] Now, what do you want? If you dare to provoke me further, draw your sword.

Sir Toby What, what! No, then I must draw an ounce or two of this bold blood from you! [*He draws his sword*]

[**Olivia** *enters*]

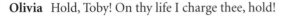

Olivia   Hold, Toby! On thy life I charge thee, hold!

40 **Sir Toby**   Madam!

Olivia   Will it be ever thus? Ungracious wretch!
   Fit for the mountains and the barbarous caves,
   Where manners ne'er were preached. Out of my sight!
   Be not offended, dear Cesario.
45   Rudesby, be gone!

                    [*Exeunt* **Sir Toby, Sir Andrew** *and* **Fabian**]

                    I prithee, gentle friend,
   Let thy fair wisdom, not thy passion, sway
   In this uncivil and unjust extent
   Against thy peace. Go with me to my house,
50   And hear thou there how many fruitless pranks
   This ruffian hath botched up, that thou thereby
   May'st smile at this. Thou shalt not choose but go;
   Do not deny. Beshrew his soul for me,
   He started one poor heart of mine in thee.

55 **Sebastian**   What relish is in this? How runs the stream?
   Or I am mad, or else this is a dream.
   Let fancy still my sense in Lethe steep;
   If it be thus to dream, still let me sleep!

Olivia   Nay; come, I prithee; would thou'dst be ruled by me!

60 **Sebastian**   Madam, I will.

Olivia   O! say so, and so be.

                                        [*Exeunt*]

190

Olivia Stop, Toby! On your life, I order you to stop!

Sir Toby Madam—

Olivia Will it always be this way? You uncouth wretch, fit only for the mountains and the barbarous caves where manners were never taught! Out of my sight! [*To* **Sebastian**] Don't be offended, dear Cesario. [*To* **Sir Toby**] Oaf! Go away!

[**Sir Toby, Sir Andrew,** *and* **Fabian** *exit*]

Please, gentle friend, let your calm wisdom, not your anger, influence you in responding to this rude and unjust assault on your peace. Come with me to my house, and there you will hear how many pointless pranks this ruffian has pulled. In that way, you might see the funny side of this one. You shall not get away; don't refuse me. Curse him [*referring to* **Sir Toby**] on my account. He alarmed my heart by alarming yours.

Sebastian What does this mean? Where is it all going? Either I've gone mad or else this is a dream. Then let imagination drown my senses in forgetfulness. If this is a dream, let me sleep forever!

Olivia Now, please come. I wish you would do as I tell you!

Sebastian Madam, I will!

Olivia Oh, be true to what you have said!

[**Olivia** *and* **Sebastian** *exit*]

Act IV

Scene II

Olivia's House. Enter **Maria** *and* **Feste**.

Maria Nay, I prithee, put on this gown and this beard; make
him believe thou art Sir Topas the curate; do it quickly; I'll call
Sir Toby the whilst.

[*Exit*]

5 **Feste** Well, I'll put it on, and I will dissemble myself in't; and
I would I were the first that ever dissembled in such a gown.
I am not tall enough to become the function well, nor lean
enough to be thought a good student; but to be said an honest
man and a good housekeeper goes as fairly as to say a careful
man and a great scholar. The competitors enter.

[*Enter* **Sir Toby Belch** *and* **Maria**]

10

Sir Toby Jove bless thee, Master Parson.

Feste Bonos dies, Sir Toby; for, as the old hermit of Prague,
that never saw pen and ink, very wittily said to a niece of
King Gorboduc, 'That that is is'; so I, being Master Parson,
15 am Master Parson, for what is 'that' but 'that', and 'is' but
'is'?

Sir Toby To him, Sir Topas.

A room in Olivia's house. **Malvolio** *is locked inside an adjacent room.* **Maria** *and* **Feste** *enter.*

Maria   Now, please put on this gown and this beard to make him believe you are Sir Topas the parson. Do it quickly. I'll go get Sir Toby meanwhile. [*She leaves*]

Feste   Well, I'll put it on, and I'll disguise myself in it. I wish I was the first person that ever masqueraded in such a gown. I am not tall enough to make a distinguished-looking parson, nor thin enough to look like a scholar. But to be called a decent man and a good host sounds as good as to be called a dutiful parson and great scholar. My fellow conspirators enter.

[**Sir Toby** *and* **Maria** *enter*]

Sir Toby   God bless you, Master Parson.

Feste   [*attempting a mock-clerical, Latin-sounding version of "good day"*] *Bonos dies,* Sir Toby. For as the old hermit of Prague, who never used pen and ink, said very cleverly to a niece of King Gorbuduc, "That that is, is." So I, being Master Parson, am Master Parson. For what is "that" but "that"? And what is "is" but "is"?

Sir Toby   Go get him, [*referring to* **Malvolio**] Sir Topas!

Feste What ho! I say. Peace in this prison.

Sir Toby The knave counterfeits well; a good knave.

Malvolio Who calls there?

20 **Feste** Sir Topas the curate, who comes to visit Malvolio the lunatic.

Malvolio Sir Topas, Sir Topas, good Sir Topas, go to my lady.

Feste Out, hyperbolical fiend! How vexest thou this man!
25 Talkest thou nothing but of ladies?

Sir Toby Well said, Master Parson.

Malvolio Sir Topas, never was man thus wronged. Good Sir Topas, do not think I am mad; they have laid me here in hideous darkness.

30 **Feste** Fie, thou dishonest man Satan! I call thee by the most modest terms; for I am one of those gentle ones that will use the devil himself with courtesy. Sayest thou that house is dark?

Malvolio As hell, Sir Topas.

35 **Feste** Why, it hath bay windows transparent as barricadoes, and the clerestories toward the south-north are as lustrous as ebony; and yet complainest thou of obstruction?

Malvolio I am not mad, Sir Topas. I say to you, this house is dark.

40 **Feste** Madman, thou errest; I say there is no darkness but ignorance, in which thou art more puzzled than the Egyptians in their fog.

Feste [*speaking in his clerical voice through the grille in the door of the room where* **Malvolio** *is confined*] Hello in there, I say. Peace be in this prison!

Sir Toby The rascal's doing a good imitation. He's a good rascal.

Malvolio [*offstage*] Who calls there?

Feste It is Sir Topas the parson, who's come to visit Malvolio the lunatic.

Malvolio Sir Topas, Sir Topas, good Sir Topas, go to my lady.

Feste [*pretending to exorcise* **Malvolio's** *"devil"*] Out, you raging fiend! How you torment this man! Can't you talk of anything but ladies?

Sir Toby Well said, Master Parson.

Malvolio Sir Topas, no man was ever mistreated as much as me. Good Sir Topas, don't believe I'm insane. *They* have confined me here in hideous darkness.

Feste For shame, you dishonest Satan! I'm calling you by the mildest terms, because I am one of those gentle ones that will treat the devil himself with courtesy. Do you say that this house is dark?

Malvolio As hell, Sir Topas.

Feste Why, it has bay windows transparent as stone walls and the high windows toward the north-south are clear as mud. And yet you're complaining that there's no light?

Malvolio I am not mad, Sir Topas. I tell you this house is dark.

Feste Madman, you are in error. I tell you there is no darkness but ignorance, in which you are more lost than the Egyptians in the Bible were in the darkness of their fog.

Malvolio I say this house is as dark as ignorance, though
ignorance were as dark as hell; and I say there was never man
45   thus abused. I am no more mad than you are; make the trial
of it in any constant question.

Feste What is the opinion of Pythagoras concerning wild
fowl?

Malvolio That the soul of our grandam might haply inhabit
50   a bird.

Feste What thinkest thou of his opinion?

Malvolio I think nobly of the soul, and no way approve his
opinion.

Feste Fare thee well; remain thou still in darkness. Thou shalt
55   hold the opinion of Pythagoras ere I will allow of thy wits,
and fear to kill a woodcock, lest thou dispossess the soul of
thy grandam. Fare thee well.

Malvolio Sir Topas! Sir Topas!

Sir Toby My most exquisite Sir Topas!

60 **Feste** Nay, I am for all waters.

Maria Thou might'st have done this without thy beard and
gown; he sees thee not.

Sir Toby To him in thine own voice, and bring me word
how thou findest him. I would we were well rid of this
65   knavery. If he may be conveniently delivered, I would he
were; for I am now so far in offence with my niece that I
cannot pursue with any safety this sport to the upshot. Come
by and by to my chamber.

[Exeunt **Sir Toby** *and* **Maria**]

Feste *[Singing]*   *Hey Robin, jolly Robin,*
70   *Tell me how thy lady does.*

Malvolio I tell you this house is as dark as ignorance, even if ignorance were as dark as hell. And I tell you that no man was ever so abused as me. I am no more insane than you are. You can test that with any reasonable question.

Feste What is the opinion of the Greek philosopher Pythagoras about wild fowl?

Malvolio That the soul of one's grandmother might perhaps inhabit a bird.

Feste What do you think of his opinion?

Malvolio I think that the soul is noble, and in no way agree with his opinion.

Feste Farewell. You must still remain in darkness. Before I will grant that you are sane, you must agree with the opinion of Pythagoras, and be afraid to kill a woodcock lest you evict the soul of your grandmother. Farewell.

Malvolio Sir Topas, Sir Topas!

Sir Toby My most expert Sir Topas!

Feste [*to* **Sir Toby**] No, I can play anybody.

Maria You could have done this role without your beard and gown; he can't see you.

Sir Toby [*to* **Feste**] Speak to him in your own voice and tell me how he is. I wish we were completely rid of this trickery. If he can be conveniently set free, I want him to be, because I am now in such deep disgrace with my niece, I cannot pursue this jest to the end with any safety. Come to my room by and by.

[**Sir Toby** *and* **Maria** *exit*]

Feste [*sings*]
    Hey, Robin, jolly Robin,
    Tell me how thy lady does.

197

Malvolio Fool!

Feste   *My lady is unkind, perdy.*

Malvolio Fool!

Feste   *Alas! why is she so?*

75 **Malvolio** Fool, I say!

Feste   *She loves another.*

                                    Who calls, ha?

Malvolio Good fool, as ever thou wilt deserve well at my
    hand, help me to a candle, and pen, ink, and paper. As I am a
80   gentleman, I will live to be thankful to thee for't.

Feste Master Malvolio!

Malvolio Ay, good fool.

Feste Alas, sir, how fell you besides your five wits?

Malvolio Fool, there was never man so notoriously abused; I
85   am as well in my wits, fool, as thou art.

Feste But as well? Then you are mad indeed, if you be no
    better in your wits than a fool.

Malvolio They have here propertied me; keep me in
    darkness, send ministers to me, asses! and do all they can to
90   face me out of my wits.

Feste Advise you what you say; the minister is here. [*As* **Sir
    Topas**] Malvolio, Malvolio, thy wits the heavens restore!
    Endeavour thyself to sleep, and leave thy vain bibble-babble.

Malvolio Sir Topas!

95 **Feste** Maintain no words with him, good fellow. [*As* **Feste**]
    Who, I, sir? Not I, sir. God be wi' you, good Sir Topas. [*As*
    Sir Topas] Marry, amen . . . [*As* **Feste**] I will, sir, I will.

Malvolio Fool!

Feste "My lady is unkind, indeed."

Malvolio Fool!

Feste "Alas, why is she so?"

Malvolio Fool, I say!

Feste "She loves another"—Who's calling, eh?

Malvolio Good fool, if you ever want to earn my gratitude, help me get a candle, and a pen, ink, and paper. As I'm a gentleman, I will indeed be thankful to you for it.

Feste Master Malvolio?

Malvolio Yes, good fool.

Feste Alas, sir, how did you come to lose your wits?

Malvolio Fool, there never was a man so scandalously abused as me. I am as sane as you are, fool.

Feste Only as sane as me? Then you are mad indeed, if you're no saner than a fool.

Malvolio They have stowed me away, keep me in darkness, send parsons to me—the asses—and do all they can to drive me out of my mind.

Feste Be careful about what you say; the parson is here. [*He speaks as* **Sir Topas**] Malvolio, Malvolio, may heaven restore your sanity! Try to sleep, and stop your silly babbling.

Malvolio Sir Topas!

Feste [*speaking as* **Sir Topas**] Don't talk with him, good fellow. [*As himself*] Who, I, sir? Not I, sir. God be with you, good Sir Topas. [*As* **Sir Topas**] Indeed, amen. [*As himself*] I will, sir, I will.

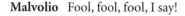

Malvolio   Fool, fool, fool, I say!

Feste   Alas, sir, be patient. What say you, sir? I am shent for
100   speaking to you.

Malvolio   Good fool, help me to some light and some paper; I
tell thee I am as well in my wits as any man in Illyria.

Feste   Well-a-day, that you were, sir!

Malvolio   By this hand, I am. Good fool, some ink, paper,
105   and light; and convey what I will set down to my lady; it shall
advantage thee more than ever the bearing of letter did.

Feste   I will help you to't. But tell me true, are you not mad
indeed, or do you but counterfeit?

Malvolio   Believe me, I am not; I tell thee true.

110 **Feste**   Nay, I'll ne'er believe a madman till I see his brains. I
will fetch you light and paper and ink.

Malvolio   Fool, I'll requite it in the highest degree; I prithee,
be gone.

Feste   [*Singing*]   *I am gone, sir,*
115   *And anon, sir,*
             I'll be with you again,
                 In a trice
                 Like to the old Vice,
             Your need to sustain;

120   *Who with dagger of lath,*
             In his rage and his wrath,
                 Cries, Ah, ha! to the devil;
             Like a mad lad,
             Pare thy nails, dad;
125   *Adieu, goodman devil.*

                                                          [*Exit*]

Malvolio Fool, fool, fool, I say!

Feste Alas, sir, be patient. What do you want? I'm scolded for speaking to you.

Malvolio Help me get some light and some paper. I tell you I am as sane as any man in Illyria.

Feste Alas, if only you were, sir.

Malvolio By this hand, I am. Good fool, some ink, paper, and light. And deliver what I write to my lady. It shall profit you more than carrying a letter ever did before.

Feste I will help you to do it. But tell me truly: Are you really insane, or are you only pretending?

Malvolio Believe me, I am not insane. I'm telling you the truth.

Feste No, I'll never believe a madman until I see his brains. I will fetch you light and paper and ink.

Malvolio Fool, I'll reward you very greatly. Please go now.

Feste [*sings*]
    I am gone, sir,
    And anon, sir,
    I'll be with you again.
    In a trice
    Like to the old Vice
    Your need to sustain.

    Who with dagger of wood
    In his rage and foul mood,
    Cries, "Bah!" to the devil;
    Like a mad lad,
    Pare thy nails, dad.
    Farewell, Master Devil!

[**Feste** *exits*]

Act IV

Scene III

Olivia's Garden. Enter **Sebastian.**

Sebastian   This is the air; that is the glorious sun;
This pearl she gave me, I do feel't and see't;
And though 'tis wonder that enwraps me thus,
Yet 'tis not madness. Where's Antonio then?
5   I could not find him at the Elephant;
Yet there he was, and there I found this credit,
That he did range the town to seek me out.
His counsel now might do me golden service;
For though my soul disputes well with my sense
10   That this may be some error, but no madness,
Yet doth this accident and flood of fortune
So far exceed all instance, all discourse,
That I am ready to distrust mine eyes,
And wrangle with my reason that persuades me
15   To any other trust but that I am mad
Or else the lady's mad; yet if 'twere so,
She could not sway her house, command her followers,
Take and give back affairs and their dispatch
With such a smooth, discreet, and stable bearing
20   As I perceive she does. There's something in't
That is deceivable. But here the lady comes.

[*Enter* **Olivia** *and a* **Priest**]

Olivia's garden. **Sebastian** *enters.*

Sebastian   This is the air; that is the glorious sun. I can see and feel this pearl she gave me. And although I am so full of wonder, I am not mad. Where's Antonio then? I could not find him at the Elephant. Yet he had been there, and I learned that they believed he had roamed through the town seeking me. His advice would be very valuable to me now. For though my reason and my senses both agree that there may be some error here, but no madness, yet this unexpected flood of good fortune so exceeds all precedent and logic that I am ready to distrust my eyes, and argue with my reason that persuades me to believe that I'm not mad. Or else my lady's mad. Yet if that were so, she could not manage her household, command her servants, take business in hand and see to its execution in such a poised, prudent, and confident manner as I see she does. There's something here I don't understand. But here comes the lady.

[**Olivia** *and a* **Priest** *enter*]

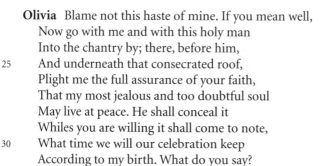

Olivia Blame not this haste of mine. If you mean well,
  Now go with me and with this holy man
  Into the chantry by; there, before him,
25 And underneath that consecrated roof,
  Plight me the full assurance of your faith,
  That my most jealous and too doubtful soul
  May live at peace. He shall conceal it
  Whiles you are willing it shall come to note,
30 What time we will our celebration keep
  According to my birth. What do you say?

Sebastian I'll follow this good man, and go with you;
  And, having sworn the truth, ever will be true.

Olivia Then lead the way, good father; and heavens so shine
35 That they may fairly note this act of mine!

[*Exeunt*]

Olivia Don't blame me for being hasty. If your intentions are good, go with me now, and with this holy man, into the chapel nearby. There, in front of him, and underneath that sacred roof, pledge that you will marry me, so that my very anxious and fearful soul may be at peace. He shall keep it secret until you are willing that it be made public, at which time we will celebrate our marriage in keeping with my rank. What do you say?

Sebastian I'll follow this good man, and go with you, and having sworn to be true, will always be so.

Olivia Then lead the way, good father, and may the heavens shine and bless this act of mine.

[**Olivia** *and* **Sebastian** *exit*]

Comprehension   Check What You Know

1. What message does Feste try to deliver to Sebastian, thinking he is Cesario?

2. How does Sebastian respond to the attacks by Sir Andrew and Sir Toby? How does Feste react?

3. Olivia chases off Sir Andrew and Sir Toby, then apologizes for them to Sebastian. How does Sebastian respond to her offer?

4. Who does Feste pretend that he is? How does he dress? Why does he have to dress up when Malvolio can't see him?

5. Feste says that Malvolio is in a bright room. How does Malvolio describe his prison?

6. Sir Toby wishes the joke were over, for two reasons. What are they?

7. After Sir Toby and Maria leave, Feste continues harassing Malvolio. What does he finally agree to give to Malvolio? Why does Malvolio want them?

8. Sebastian is in a tizzy. Why does he believe that Olivia is mad? Why does he believe that she is sane? Whose advice does he wish he had?

9. What does Olivia want to do? Why does Sebastian agree?

Activities & Role-Playing   Classes or Book Clubs

There's Irony . . . and Then There's Lying . . .   Irony is saying one thing and meaning another. For instance, you say, "Yes, that's a great looking outfit" to your friend. She says, "Thanks," and goes to change clothes. Your friend knew you weren't serious—that you meant that the outfit was terrible. Were you lying? No, because your friend *knows* that you're being ironic. What about in Act 3, when Fabian praises Andrew's letter? Is he lying? The audience knows what he means, so for them he's being ironic. Sir Andrew doesn't know, so for him Fabian is lying. We don't judge Fabian harshly for a number of reasons. For instance, the joke isn't serious. It succeeds because Andrew isn't very smart, and the irony is funny.

Look at Scene 2. Feste puts on a robe and pretends that he is a

©Hulton-Deutsch Collection/CORBIS

clergyman, Sir Topas. Malvolio believes the charade, but we know what is happening. Is this irony? Has it crossed over into something harsher, something more cruel? Discuss this scene and others where irony is a factor.

This Is Amazing! In Scene 3, lines 1–21, Sebastian tries to figure out what is going on. He goes through many emotions—confusion, wonder, curiosity, desire for a friend's advice, and reasonable questions of his own sanity. Working with a small group, read through the speech. Then analyze Sebastian's confused feelings. What ideas about love does he reveal in his speech? Are his feelings familiar? What do you think of his final decision?

Discussion Classes or Book Clubs

1. Maria and Toby recruit Feste to help bedevil Malvolio as he sits in his prison. Why does Feste go along with the joke? Why does he continue to torment Malvolio after everyone else has left?

2. If you were Sebastian's friend, what advice would you give to him? Should he accept his good luck and go along with Olivia? Or should he try to convince her of her mistake? Should he try to slow things down so that he knows her a little better before they marry?

3. Malvolio is an unpleasant fellow whose view of life is completely out of step with the views of everyone else in the play. The world of Illyria is festive, and love is the primary concern. Malvolio isn't interested in either. Most people are okay with the idea that he needs his comeuppance. But many commentators think that the punishment goes too far. Do you agree? List the reasons why Malvolio deserves his punishment. Then discuss whether the punishment he receives is appropriate.

Suggestions for Writing Improve Your Skills

1. At the beginning of Act 3, Scene 1, Viola and Feste meet and talk together for a while. Then, at the beginning of Act 4, Scene 1, Sebastian and Feste meet and talk together. Read both meetings. Then pretend that you are Feste and are writing a letter to a friend, describing the confusing meetings. In the letter, compare "Cesario 1" and "Cesario 2." Begin with their appearance. Then describe how they talk—do they use the same kinds of phrases? How are their attitudes alike? How are they different?

2. After Sir Topas's first meeting with Malvolio, Sir Toby says that he wishes this bit of fun were over with. He is already in enough trouble with Olivia from the attack on Cesario (he actually attacked Sebastian, although Toby doesn't know it). Have you ever had something very simple and innocent grow into something that you didn't anticipate and didn't want to have happen? Write an essay about your "From Bad to Worse" adventure.

All the World's a Stage   Introduction

So, Sebastian has declared he will marry Olivia. Olivia, priest at the ready, is ecstatic, unaware that the person she's marrying is *not* the person she fell in love with. Who knows what the Duke will do when he finds out? Viola, who knows her brother may be alive, doesn't know that he has now married Olivia. Sir Toby and Sir Andrew may still be trying to embroil Cesario in a duel with Sir Andrew, in which either man could be injured or even killed. Malvolio is being held in a dark room as a madman. Antonio, who believes Sebastian has denied his friendship, has been arrested for earlier acts of piracy and may be executed. How is all this going to work out?

What's in a Name?   Characters

Twelfth Night is full of pairs and mismatches in love.
- **Duke Orsino:** with Olivia (a mismatch because she doesn't love him in return) and with Cesario (a mismatch because he's actually a she)
- **Olivia:** with Cesario (a mismatch because he's actually a she) and with Sebastian (an uncertain match)
- **Olivia:** also paired with Malvolio, although her interpretation of the match (he is a servant) is not the same as his (she might become his wife)
- **Sebastian:** with Olivia (much to his amazement) and with Antonio (a mismatch because their friendship has landed Antonio in jail)
- **Sir Toby:** with Sir Andrew (a mismatch because it enables Toby to take advantage of Andrew) and with Maria (an uncertain match)

Now all the mismatches must be resolved. A tall order, indeed. In fact, it is so difficult that we will hear about some people but never see them again.

COME WHAT MAY   Things to Watch For

Olivia and Sebastian married so quickly that they may as well have eloped. Nonetheless, the marriage won't remain a secret. What will happen the next time Cesario appears at Olivia's household? Has the Duke done anything in the past to suggest how he might react when he learns that the woman he loves so madly is married to someone else? Is there a chance of violence?

Violence doesn't seem likely—this is a comedy, after all—but there has been an undercurrent of it throughout the play. The conflict between Malvolio and everyone in the household took on a vicious edge when he threatened to have Maria dismissed. The duel between Sir Andrew and Cesario became suddenly, frighteningly real when Andrew thought he was confronting Cesario and instead attacked Sebastian. And although Malvolio deserves to be brought down a peg or two, the way he is treated is beginning to cross the line between good-natured gulling and something much more cruel.

Symbolic of the edgy situation, Sir Toby and Sir Andrew will appear very early in Act 5—covered with blood.

All Our Yesterdays Historical and Social Context

With everything that's going on, you might start wondering if *Twelfth Night* really is a comedy. The answer is yes. Comedies are more than just jokes and pratfalls. When we watch a comedy, we know that it is *not* realistic. No matter how serious problems may seem, at the end they are magically resolved. We know everything is going to work out—we just aren't sure how. Our enjoyment comes from watching the author resolve the puzzles.

When Olivia and Sebastian "marry," they don't go through a formal wedding ceremony. That will come later. During Shakespeare's time, before the actual marriage there was a ceremony in which the man and woman pledged themselves to marry. The closest thing to this today is an engagement, but an engagement is not as legally binding as the Elizabethan pledge.

The Play's the Thing Staging

Twelfth Night has all the characteristics of a comedy. Human nature is the primary source of the fun. Also, Shakespeare's audiences expected to see certain characters in a comedy, and they're here, such as the pining lovers, the boisterous drunkard, the noble warrior, the witty fool, and the clever servant. The plot also includes the standard comic fare: dancing, singing, mock battles, confused identities, eavesdropping, and practical jokes.

But there is a sad, almost melancholy undertone in *Twelfth Night.* Sprinkled throughout the events are sad songs about lost youth and lost love. Older characters seem to be especially aware of loss. Even Sir Andrew remarks wistfully, "I was adored once too." Under all the fun, there seems to be an awareness that love and joy cannot last. For this reason, most commentators say *Twelfth Night* belongs with Shakespeare's more mature and complex later plays.

My Words Fly Up Language

It's time for language of discovery. How do you think Viola and Sebastian will behave when they discover one another? How will other people account for the fact that Viola fooled them completely? Watch for the subtle back-and-forth between the twins when they finally meet.

At another point the Duke refers to "a natural perspective." This is a reference to an optical illusion, caused by what was called a perspective glass. When you looked at an object through the glass, its appearance was changed.

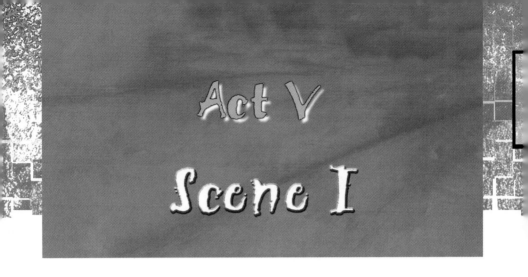

Act V

Scene I

Before Olivia's House. Enter **Feste** *and* **Fabian.**

Fabian Now, as thou lovest me, let me see his letter.

Feste Good Master Fabian, grant me another request.

Fabian Anything.

Feste Do not desire to see this letter.

5 **Fabian** This is, to give a dog, and in recompense desire my dog again.

      [*Enter* **Duke, Viola, Curio,** *and* **Attendants**]

Duke Belong you to the Lady Olivia, friends?

Feste Ay, sir; we are some of her trappings.

Duke I know thee well; how dost thou, my good fellow?

10 **Feste** Truly, sir, the better for my foes and the worse for my friends.

Duke Just the contrary; the better for thy friends.

Feste No, sir, the worse.

Duke How can that be?

15 **Feste** Marry, sir, they praise me and make an ass of me; now my foes tell me plainly I am an ass; so that by my foes, sir, I profit in the knowledge of myself, and by my friends I am

In front of Olivia's house. **Feste** *and* **Fabian** *enter.*

Fabian If you're my friend, now let me see Malvolio's letter.

Feste Good Master Fabian, grant me a request in return.

Fabian Anything.

Feste Don't ask to see this letter.

Fabian This is like giving me a dog and in return asking for the dog back.

   [*The* **Duke, Viola, Curio,** *and* **Attendants** *enter*]

Duke Do you belong to the Lady Olivia, friends?

Feste Yes, sir, we are part of her household.

Duke I know you well; how do you do, my good fellow?

Feste Truly, sir, the better because of my enemies and the worse because of my friends.

Duke Just the opposite: the better because of your friends.

Feste No sir, the worse.

Duke How can that be?

Feste Indeed sir, my friends praise me and make a fool of me. Now my enemies tell me plainly I am a fool. So that by my enemies I profit in the knowledge of myself; but by my friends

abused; so that, conclusions to be as kisses, if your four
negatives make your two affirmatives, why then, the worse
20   for my friends and the better for my foes.

Duke Why, this is excellent.

Feste By my troth, sir, no; though it please you to be one of
my friends.

Duke Thou shalt not be the worse for me; there's gold.

25   **Feste** But that it would be double-dealing, sir, I would you
could make it another.

Duke O! you give me ill counsel.

Feste Put your grace in your pocket, sir, for this once, and let
your flesh and blood obey it.

30   **Duke** Well, I will be so much a sinner to be a double-dealer;
there's another.

Feste Primo, secundo, tertio, is a good play; and the old
saying is, the third pays for all; the triplex, sir, is a good
tripping measure; or the bells of Saint Bennet, sir, may put
35   you in mind: one, two, three.

Duke You can fool no more money out of me at this throw; if
you will let your lady know I am here to speak with her, and
bring her along with you, it may awake my bounty further.

Feste Marry, sir, lullaby to your bounty till I come again. I
40   go, sir; but I would not have you to think that my desire of
having is the sin of covetousness; but as you say, sir, let your
bounty take a nap; I will awake it anon.

[*Exit*]

Viola Here comes the man, sir, that did rescue me.

[*Enter* **Antonio** *and* **Officers**]

I am deceived. Conclusions are like kisses: so if a girl's four "no's" are equal to two "yeses," then I'm the worse because of my friends, and the better because of my enemies.

Duke Very clever.

Feste Indeed, sir, no. Though you're kind enough to be one of my friends.

Duke You shall not be the worse for me. [*He gives him a coin*] Here's gold.

Feste Except that it would be double-dealing, I wish you could give me another.

Duke Oh, you're giving me bad advice.

Feste Put your virtue in your pocket this once, sir, and obey your human nature.

Duke I will sin so far as to be a double-dealer. [*He gives him another coin*] Here's another.

Feste "One, two, three" is a good game, and the old saying says, "Third time lucky." Triple time in music, sir, is a good, quick beat, or perhaps the bells of St. Benedict's might remind you—one, two, three.

Duke You can't fool any more money out of me this time. If you will let your lady know I am here to speak with her, and bring her back with you, it might reawaken my generosity.

Feste Indeed, sir, may your generosity sleep well till I return. I go, sir, but I would not have you think that my desire to have is the sin of greed. But as you say, sir, let your generosity take a nap. I will awaken it soon.

[**Feste** *exits*]

Viola [*to the* **Duke**] Here comes the man that rescued me, sir.

[**Antonio** *and the* **Officers** *enter*]

Duke That face of his I do remember well;
45   Yet, when I saw it last, it was besmeared
    As black as Vulcan in the smoke of war.
    A baubling vessel was he captain of,
    For shallow draught and bulk unprizable;
    With which such scathful grapple did he make
50   With the most noble bottom of our fleet,
    That very envy and the tongue of loss
    Cried fame and honour on him. What's the matter?

1st Officer Orsino, this is that Antonio
    That took the Phoenix and her fraught from Candy;
55   And this is he that did the Tiger board,
    When your young nephew Titus lost his leg.
    Here in the streets, desperate of shame and state,
    In private brabble did we apprehend him.

Viola He did me kindness, sir, drew on my side;
60   But in conclusion put strange speech upon me;
    I know not what 'twas but distraction.

Duke Notable pirate! thou salt-water thief!
    What foolish boldness brought thee to their mercies,
    Whom thou, in terms so bloody and so dear,
65   Hast made thine enemies?

Antonio   Orsino, noble sir,
    Be pleased that I shake off these names you give me;
    Antonio never yet was thief or pirate,
    Though I confess, on base and ground enough,
70   Orsino's enemy. A witchcraft drew me hither;
    That most ungrateful boy there by your side,
    From the rude sea's enraged and foamy mouth
    Did I redeem; a wreck past hope he was;
    His life I gave him, and did thereto add
75   My love, without retention or restraint,
    All his in dedication; for his sake
    Did I expose myself, pure for his love,

Duke That face of his I remember well. But when I last saw it, it was smeared as black with the smoke of battle as the fire god Vulcan's. He was captain of a tiny vessel, of no value as a prize because of its shallow draft and small size. With it he made such a damaging attack on the best ship of our fleet that, despite our ill will and loss, we proclaimed his fame and honor. What's he done?

1st Officer Orsino, this is the Antonio that took the *Phoenix* and her cargo as she returned from Crete. He is the one who boarded the *Tiger,* when your young nephew Titus lost his leg. We arrested him here in the streets, as he recklessly ignored both shame and danger in a private brawl.

Viola He was kind to me, sir. He drew his sword in my defense, but then spoke very strangely to me. I don't know what it meant, unless he's mad.

Duke [*to* **Antonio**] You notorious pirate and sea-faring thief! What foolish boldness brought you to the mercy of those whom you have made your enemies in such bloody and costly ways?

Antonio Orsino, noble sir, permit me to refute these names you give me. Antonio has never been a thief or pirate; although I will confess, for obvious reasons, to being Orsino's enemy. An enchantment drew me here. I rescued from the rough sea's angry waters that most ungrateful boy that stands by your side. He had no hope of surviving. I gave him his life, and added to that my love, offered without reservation or restraint, and dedicated completely to him. For

Into the danger of this adverse town;
Drew to defend him when he was beset;
80 Where being apprehended, his false cunning,
Not meaning to partake with me in danger,
Taught him to face me out of his acquaintance,
And grew a twenty-years-removed thing
While one would wink; denied me mine own purse,
85 Which I had recommended to his use
Not half an hour before.

Viola   How can this be?

Duke When came he to this town?

Antonio Today, my lord; and for three months before,
90 No interim, not a minute's vacancy
Both day and night did we keep company.

[*Enter* **Olivia** *and* **Attendants**]

Duke Here comes the countess; now heaven walks on earth!
But for thee, fellow: fellow, thy words are madness;
Three months this youth hath tended upon me;
95 But more of that anon. Take him aside.

Olivia What would my lord, but that he may not have,
Wherein Olivia may seem serviceable?
Cesario, you do not keep promise with me.

Viola Madam?

100 **Duke** Gracious Olivia –

Olivia What do you say, Cesario? Good my lord, –

Viola My lord would speak; my duty hushes me.

Olivia If it be aught to the old tune, my lord,
It is as fat and fulsome to mine ear,
105 As howling after music.

his sake, and purely for love of him, I put myself into danger in this hostile town. I drew my sword to defend him when he was attacked. When I was arrested, since he did not intend to share my danger, his treacherous cunning prompted him to deny that he knew me. And before you could wink an eye, he became like someone who had not seen me for twenty years. He refused me my own purse, which I had given to him for his use not half an hour before.

Viola How can this be?

Duke [*to the* **Officers**] When did he come to this town?

Antonio Today, my lord, and for the past three months, without the space of a moment intervening, we have been together both day and night.

[**Olivia** *and her* **Attendants** *enter*]

Duke Here comes the countess. Now heaven walks on earth! [*To* **Antonio**] But as for you fellow—fellow, your words are madness. For the past three months this youth has attended me. But more of that later. [*To the* **Officers**] Take him over there.

Olivia [*to the* **Duke**] What does my lord wish—except that which he cannot have—in which Olivia might show her duty? [*To* **Viola**] Cesario, you are not keeping your promise to me.

Viola Madam?

Duke Gracious Olivia—

Olivia What do you say, Cesario? [*To quiet the* **Duke** *while she listens to* **Viola**] Please, my lord—

Viola My lord wishes to speak; duty requires I stay silent.

Olivia If it is in any way the old love song, my lord, it is as gross and distasteful to my ear as howling to music.

Duke   Still so cruel?

Olivia Still so constant, lord.

Duke What, to perverseness? You uncivil lady,
    To whose ingrate and unauspicious altars
110 My soul the faithfull'st offerings hath breathed out
    That e'er devotion tendered! What shall I do?

Olivia Even what it please my lord, that shall become him.

Duke Why should I not, had I the heart to do it,
    Like to the Egyptian thief at point of death,
115 Kill what I love? A savage jealousy
    That sometimes savours nobly. But hear me this:
    Since you to non-regardance cast my faith,
    And that I partly know the instrument
    That screws me from my true place in your favour,
120 Live you the marble-breasted tyrant still;
    But this your minion, whom I know you love,
    And whom, by heaven I swear, I tender dearly,
    Him will I tear out of that cruel eye,
    Where he sits crowned in his master's spite.
125 [*To* **Viola**] Come, boy, with me; my thoughts are ripe in
        mischief;
    I'll sacrifice the lamb that I do love,
    To spite a raven's heart within a dove.

Viola And I, most jocund, apt, and willingly,
130 To do you rest, a thousand deaths would die.

Olivia Where goes Cesario?

Viola   After him I love
    More than I love these eyes, more than my life,
    More, by all mores, than e'er I shall love wife.
135 If I do feign, you witnesses above,
    Punish my life for tainting of my love!

Olivia Ay me, detested! how am I beguiled!

Duke Still so cruel?

Olivia Still so faithful, my lord.

Duke What, to perverseness? You rude lady, to whose ungrateful and unfavorable altars my soul has spoken the most faithful prayers that devotion ever offered! What shall I do?

Olivia Whatever my lord wishes, that will suit his position.

Duke Why shouldn't I—if I had the heart to do it—kill what I love, like the Egyptian thief facing death who wanted to kill the captive he had fallen in love with. Such savage jealousy sometimes has a noble quality about it. But listen to this: since you neglect and cast aside my faithful love, and since I think I know what has forced me from my rightful place in your favor, remain the stony-hearted tyrant always. But this darling [*indicating* **Viola**] of yours, whom I know you love, and whom—I swear by heaven—I value highly, him I will snatch away from your cruel sight, where he is admired instead of his master. [*To* **Viola**] Come with me, boy, my mind is ready to do injury. I'll sacrifice the lamb [*referring to* **Viola**] that I love, to spite the raven's savage heart [*referring to* **Olivia**] that lives within a dove.

Viola And I am most joyful, ready, and willing to die a thousand deaths to give you peace.

Olivia Where is Cesario going?

Viola To follow the man I love, more than I love my eyes, more than my life, more by all such comparisons than I shall ever love a wife. If I don't mean it, you heavens above, take my life for being false to my love!

Olivia Alas, how I'm despised, how I'm misled!

Viola Who does beguile you? Who does do you wrong?

Olivia Hast thou forgot thyself? Is it so long?
140   Call forth the holy father.

Duke   Come away!

Olivia Whither, my lord? Cesario, husband, stay.

Duke Husband!

Olivia   Ay, husband; can he that deny?

145 **Duke** Her husband, sirrah!

Viola   No, my lord, not I.

Olivia Alas! it is the baseness of thy fear
        That makes thee strangle thy propriety.
        Fear not, Cesario; take thy fortunes up;
150   Be that thou know'st thou art, and then thou art
        As great as that thou fear'st.

        [*Enter* **Priest**]

                                O welcome, father!
        Father, I charge thee, by thy reverence,
        Here to unfold, though lately we intended
155   To keep in darkness what occasion now
        Reveals before 'tis ripe, what thou dost know
        Hath newly passed between this youth and me.

Priest A contract of eternal bond of love,
        Confirmed by mutual joinder of your hands,
160   Attested by the holy close of lips,
        Strengthened by interchangement of your rings;
        And all the ceremony of this compact

220

Viola Who misleads you? Who does you wrong?

Olivia Have you forgotten yourself? Is it so long? [*To an* **Attendant**] Call the holy priest here.

[**Attendant** *exits*]

Duke [*to* **Viola**] Come away!

Olivia [*to* **Orsino**] Where, my lord? [*To* **Viola**] Cesario, my husband, stay.

Duke Husband?

Olivia Yes, husband. Can he deny it?

Duke [*to* **Viola**] Her husband, boy?

Viola No my lord, not I.

Olivia Alas, it's your cowardly fear that makes you deny your identity as my husband. Don't be afraid, Cesario. Seize your fortunes. Be what you know you are, and then you will be as great as him [*referring to the* **Duke**] you fear.

[*The* **Attendant** *and the* **Priest** *enter*]

Oh welcome, father! Father, I order you by your priesthood, to disclose here—although we intended to keep secret what circumstances have now revealed prematurely—what you know has recently taken place between this youth and me.

Priest A contract of an eternal union of love, acknowledged by joining your hands, shown in a holy kiss, strengthened by the exchange of your rings, and all the ceremony of this

Sealed in my function, by my testimony;
Since when, my watch hath told me, toward my grave
165   I have travelled but two hours.

Duke O thou dissembling cub! what wilt thou be
When time hath sowed a grizzle on thy case?
Or will not else thy craft so quickly grow
That thine own trip shall be thine overthrow?
170   Farewell, and take her; but direct thy feet
Where thou and I henceforth may never meet.

Viola My lord, I do protest, –

Olivia   O! do not swear;
Hold little faith, though thou hast too much fear.

[*Enter* **Sir Andrew Aguecheek**]

175   **Sir Andrew** For the love of God, a surgeon! Send one
presently to Sir Toby.

Olivia What's the matter?

Sir Andrew He has broke my head across, and has given Sir
Toby a bloody coxcomb too. For the love of God, your help!
180   I had rather than forty pound I were at home.

Olivia Who has done this, Sir Andrew?

Sir Andrew The count's gentleman, one Cesario; we took him
for a coward, but he's the very devil incardinate.

Duke My gentleman, Cesario?

185   **Sir Andrew** 'Od's lifelings! here he is. You broke my head
for nothing! And that that I did, I was set on to do't by
Sir Toby.

Viola Why do you speak to me? I never hurt you;
You drew your sword upon me without cause;
190   But I bespake you fair, and hurt you not.

betrothal approved and witnessed by me as priest. Since that time, my watch tells me, two hours have passed of my journey to the grave.

Duke [*to* **Viola**] Oh, you false cub! What will you be like when age has turned your muzzle gray? Or will your cunning grow so quickly that you'll trip yourself up? Farewell, and take her, but direct your steps so that you and I will never meet again.

Viola My lord, I swear—

Olivia Oh, don't swear! Keep a little of your promise, even though you are so fearful.

[**Sir Andrew** *enters*]

Sir Andrew For the love of God, a surgeon! Send one to Sir Toby at once!

Olivia What's the matter?

Sir Andrew He has cut my head open, and has given Sir Toby a bloody crown too. For the love of God, help us! I would give a lot of money to be at home now.

Olivia Who has done this, Sir Andrew?

Sir Andrew The Count's attendant, the one named Cesario. We thought he was a coward, but he's the devil himself!

Duke My attendant Cesario?

Sir Andrew Good heavens, here he is! [*To* **Viola**] You broke my head for no reason. What I did, Sir Toby put me up to.

Viola Why speak to me? I never hurt you. You drew your sword on me for no reason. But I spoke politely to you, and didn't hurt you.

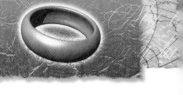

Sir Andrew If a bloody coxcomb be a hurt, you have hurt me; I think you set nothing by a bloody coxcomb.

[*Enter* **Sir Toby** *and* **Feste**]

Here comes Sir Toby halting; you shall hear more; but if he had not been in drink he would have tickled you othergates
195   than he did.

Duke How now, gentleman! how is't with you?

Sir Toby That's all one; has hurt me, and there's the end on't. Sot, didst see Dick Surgeon, sot?

Feste O! he's drunk, Sir Toby, an hour agone; his eyes were
200   set at eight i' the morning.

Sir Toby Then he's a rogue, and a passy-measures pavin. I hate a drunken rogue.

Olivia Away with him! Who hath made this havoc with them?

205 **Sir Andrew** I'll help you, Sir Toby, because we'll be dressed together.

Sir Toby Will you help? An ass-head, and a coxcomb, and a knave, a thin-faced knave, a gull!

Olivia Get him to bed, and let his hurt be looked to.

[*Exeunt* **Feste, Fabian, Sir Toby** *and* **Sir Andrew**]

[*Enter* **Sebastian**]

210 **Sebastian** I am sorry, madam, I have hurt your kinsman;
But had it been the brother of my blood,
I must have done no less with wit and safety.
You throw a strange regard upon me, and by that
I do perceive it hath offended you;
215   Pardon me, sweet one, even for the vows
We made each other but so late ago.

Sir Andrew If a bloody crown is a hurt, you have hurt me. I
believe you think nothing of a bloody crown. Here comes Sir
Toby limping—you shall hear more of this. If only he hadn't
been drunk, he'd have beaten you otherwise than he did.

[**Sir Toby** *and* **Feste** *enter*]

Duke [*To* **Sir Toby**] How are you, sir? How are you doing?

Sir Toby It's no matter. He has wounded me, and that's that.
[*To* **Feste**] Fool, have you seen Dick the Surgeon, fool?

Feste Oh, he was drunk an hour ago, Sir Toby. He passed out
at eight this morning.

Sir Toby Then he's a rogue and a slow-moving one. I hate a
drunken rogue.

Olivia Take him away. Who has hurt them this way?

Sir Andrew I'll help you, Sir Toby, because we'll have our
wounds cared for together.

Sir Toby Help from *you*—an ass-head, a fool, and a rascal—a
thin-faced rascal—a dupe?

Olivia Get him to bed, and see that his injuries are treated.

[**Sir Toby, Sir Andrew, Feste,** *and* **Fabian** *exit*]

[**Sebastian** *enters*]

Sebastian I am sorry, madam, I have wounded your kinsman;
but had he been my own brother I could have done nothing
else with a reasonable concern for my safety. You're looking
at me like a stranger, and from that I see that I have offended
you. Pardon me, sweet one, because of the vows we made
each other so recently.

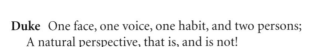

Duke One face, one voice, one habit, and two persons;
A natural perspective, that is, and is not!

Sebastian Antonio! O my dear Antonio!
220 How have the hours racked and tortured me
Since I have lost thee!

Antonio Sebastian are you?

Sebastian   Fear'st thou that, Antonio?

Antonio How have you made division of yourself?
225 An apple cleft in two is not more twin
Than these two creatures. Which is Sebastian?

Olivia Most wonderful!

Sebastian Do I stand there? I never had a brother;
Nor can there be that deity in my nature,
230 Of here and everywhere. I had a sister,
Whom the blind waves and surges have devoured.
Of charity, what kin are you to me?
What countryman, what name, what parentage?

Viola Of Messaline; Sebastian was my father;
235 Such a Sebastian was my brother too,
So went he suited to his watery tomb.
If spirits can assume both form and suit
You come to fright us.

Sebastian   A spirit I am indeed;
240 But am in that dimension grossly clad
Which from the womb I did participate.
Were you a woman, as the rest goes even,
I should my tears let fall upon your cheek,
And say 'Thrice welcome, drowned Viola!'

245 **Viola** My father had a mole upon his brow.

Sebastian And so had mine.

Duke [*looking at* **Sebastian** *and* **Viola**] One face, one voice, one way of dressing, and two persons; an optical illusion that's real, that is and is not!

Sebastian Antonio! Oh my dear Antonio! How very painful the hours have been since I lost you!

Antonio Are you Sebastian?

Sebastian Do you doubt it, Antonio?

Antonio Have you divided yourself in two? An apple, cut in half, is not more alike than these two creatures. Which is Sebastian?

Olivia Most wonderful!

Sebastian [*seeing* **Viola**] Do I stand there? I never had a brother. Nor do I have a godlike power of being in two places at once. I had a sister, who was drowned by the unfeeling waves. [*To* **Viola**] If you'd be so kind: how are you related to me? What's your country? What's your name? Who are your parents?

Viola I'm from Messaline. Sebastian was my father's name. Sebastian was my brother's name too. He was dressed like you when he was drowned. If spirits can take on both body and clothing, you have come to frighten us.

Sebastian I am a spirit indeed, but still clothed in the body which I've had since I was born. If you were a woman, since everything else about you agrees, I'd weep upon your cheek and say over and over again, "Welcome, drowned Viola."

Viola My father had a mole on his brow.

Sebastian And so had mine.

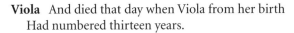

Viola And died that day when Viola from her birth
 Had numbered thirteen years.

Sebastian O! that record is lively in my soul.
250 He finished indeed his mortal act
 That day that made my sister thirteen years.

Viola If nothing lets to make us happy both,
 But this my masculine usurped attire,
 Do not embrace me till each circumstance
255 Of place, time, fortune, do cohere and jump
 That I am Viola; which to confirm,
 I'll bring you to a captain in this town,
 Where lie my maiden weeds; by whose gentle help
 I was preserved to serve this noble count.
260 All the occurrence of my fortune since
 Hath been between this lady and this lord.

Sebastian So comes it, lady, you have been mistook,
 But nature to her bias drew in that.
 You would have been contracted to a maid;
265 Nor are you there, by my life, deceived.
 You are betrothed both to a maid and man.

Duke Be not amazed; right noble is his blood.
 If this be so, as yet the glass seems true,
 I shall have share in this most happy wreck.
270 Boy, thou hast said to me a thousand times
 Thou never should'st love woman like to me.

Viola And all those sayings will I over-swear,
 And all those swearings keep as true in soul
 As doth that orbed continent the fire
275 That severs day from night.

Duke   Give me thy hand;
 And let me see thee in thy woman's weeds.

Viola And my father died on the day when Viola became thirteen years old.

Sebastian Oh, that memory is vivid in my mind! He indeed ended his mortal life the day my sister became thirteen years old.

Viola If nothing hinders us both from being happy but this male dress I've taken as a disguise, do not embrace me until every circumstance of place, time, and chance comes together and proves that I am Viola. To confirm this, I'll take you to a captain in this town, at whose house are my woman's clothes. By his kind help I was saved, to serve this noble count. Since then, all that has happened to me has involved this lady and this lord.

Sebastian [*to* **Olivia**] That is how it happened, lady, that you were mistaken. But nature sent you in the right direction. You would have been married to a young woman who was chaste; and, upon my life, you haven't been deceived in that. You're betrothed to a chaste man.

Duke [*to* **Olivia**] Don't be upset. He's clearly of noble blood. If this optical illusion proves to be real, I shall have a share in this most fortunate shipwreck. [*To* **Viola**] Boy, you have said to me a thousand times that you would never love a woman as much as you love me.

Viola And all those things I said I will swear to again, and I will keep all those oaths as truly in my soul as the sun rises to separate day from night.

Duke Give me your hand, and let me see you in your woman's clothes.

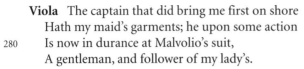

Viola The captain that did bring me first on shore
Hath my maid's garments; he upon some action
280 Is now in durance at Malvolio's suit,
A gentleman, and follower of my lady's.

Olivia He shall enlarge him. Fetch Malvolio hither.
And yet, alas, now I remember me,
They say, poor gentleman, he is much distract.
285 A most extracting frenzy of mine own
From my remembrance clearly banished his.

[*Enter* **Feste,** *with a letter, and* **Fabian**]

How does he, sirrah?

Feste Truly, madam, he holds Belzebub at the stave's end as
well as a man in his case may do. Has here writ a letter to you;
290 I should have given it you today morning; but as a madman's
epistles are no gospels, so it skills not much when they are
delivered.

Olivia Open't, and read it.

Feste Look then to be well edified when the fool delivers the
295 madman. [*Reads*] By the Lord, madam, –

Olivia How now! art thou mad?

Feste No, madam, I do but read madness; an your ladyship
will have it as it ought to be, you must allow vox.

Olivia Prithee, read i' thy right wits.

300 **Feste** So I do, madonna; but to read his right wits is to read
thus; therefore perpend, my princess, and give ear.

Olivia [*To* **Fabian**] Read it you, sirrah.

Viola The captain that first brought me ashore has my female garments. He is now in prison upon some charge brought by Malvolio, a gentleman and attendant of my lady's.

Olivia He shall release him. Bring Malvolio here. And yet, alas, I now remember that they say the poor gentleman is out of his mind. A very distracting madness of my own banished his madness from my memory.

[**Feste,** *carrying a letter, enters with* **Fabian**]

[*To* **Feste**] How is he, fellow?

Feste He keeps the devil at arm's length as well as a man in his condition can. He has written this letter to you. I should have given it to you this morning. But as a madman's letters are not gospel truth, it doesn't matter much when they're delivered.

Olivia Open it and read it.

Feste You can expect to be enlightened when the fool speaks the words of the madman. [*He reads in a raving voice*] "By the Lord, madam"—

Olivia What's this, are you mad as well?

Feste No, madam, I'm only reading madness. If your ladyship wants to hear it as it should sound, you must allow me to do the appropriate voice.

Olivia Please read as if you were in your right mind.

Feste That's what I'm doing, my lady. But to read his right mind is to read in this way. Therefore pay attention, my princess, and listen.

Olivia [*to* **Fabian**] You read it, fellow.

Fabian [*Reading*] 'By the Lord, madam, you wrong me, and
the world shall know it; though you have put me into
305 darkness, and given your drunken cousin rule over me, yet
have I the benefit of my senses as well as your ladyship. I
have your own letter that induced me to the semblance I put
on; with the which I doubt not but to do myself much right,
or you much shame. Think of me as you please. I leave my
310 duty a little unthought of, and speak out of my injury.
The Madly-used Malvolio'

Olivia Did he write this?

Feste Ay, madam.

Duke This savours not much of distraction.

315 **Olivia** See him delivered, Fabian; bring him hither.

[*Exit* **Fabian**]

My lord, so please you, these things further thought on,
To think me as well a sister as a wife,
One day shall crown the alliance on't, so please you,
Here at my house and at my proper cost.

320 **Duke** Madam, I am most apt to embrace your offer.
[*To* **Viola**] Your master quits you; and for your service done
him,
So much against the mettle of your sex,
So far beneath your soft and tender breeding,
325 And since you called me master for so long,
Here is my hand; you shall from this time be
Your master's mistress.

Olivia   A sister! You are she.

[*Enter* **Fabian** *with* **Malvolio**]

Duke Is this the madman?

Fabian [*reads*] "By the Lord, madam, you do me wrong, and the world shall know of it. Although you have put me in a dark room, and given your drunken cousin power over me, yet I am as sane as your ladyship. I have your own letter that influenced me to act as I did. With this letter I can surely put myself in the right and put you to shame. Think what you like of me. I am forgetting my duty to you a little, but speak from my sense of injury.

The Madly Used Malvolio"

Olivia Did he write this?

Feste Yes, madam.

Duke This doesn't sound like madness.

Olivia See that he's released, Fabian. Bring him here.

[**Fabian** *exits*]

[*To the* **Duke**] My lord, I hope it pleases you—when you have given further thought to these things—to think as well of me as a sister as you would have as a wife. If it pleases you, one double wedding shall celebrate this alliance here at my house and at my own expense.

Duke Madam, I am very ready to accept your offer. [*To* **Viola**] Your master frees you. And for the service you have done him—which was so much against your woman's nature and so far beneath your gentle upbringing—and since you called me "master" for so long, here is my hand. You shall from this time on be your master's wife.

Olivia [*to* **Viola**] A sister! You are she!

[**Fabian** *enters with* **Malvolio**]

Duke Is this the madman?

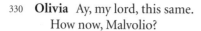

330 **Olivia** Ay, my lord, this same.
  How now, Malvolio?

Malvolio Madam, you have done me wrong,
  Notorious wrong.

Olivia   Have I, Malvolio? No.

335 **Malvolio** Lady, you have. Pray you peruse that letter.
  You must not now deny it is your hand;
  Write from it, if you can, in hand or phrase;
  Or say 'tis not your seal nor your invention;
  You can say none of this. Well, grant it then,
340 And tell me, in the modesty of honour,
  Why you have given me such clear lights of favour
  Bade me come smiling and cross-gartered to you,
  To put on yellow stockings, and to frown
  Upon Sir Toby and the lighter people;
345 And, acting this in an obedient hope,
  Why have you suffered me to be imprisoned,
  Kept in a dark house, visited by the priest,
  And made the most notorious geck and gull
  That e'er invention played on? Tell me why.

350 **Olivia** Alas, Malvolio, this is not my writing,
  Though, I confess, much like the character;
  But, out of question, 'tis Maria's hand;
  And now I do bethink me, it was she
  First told me thou wast mad; then cam'st in smiling,
355 And in such forms which here were presupposed
  Upon thee in the letter. Prithee, be content;
  This practice hath most shrewdly passed upon thee;
  But when we know the grounds and authors of it,
  Thou shalt be both the plantiff and the judge
360 Of thine own cause.

  Fabian   Good madam, hear me speak,
  And let no quarrel nor no brawl to come
  Taint the condition of this present hour,
  Which I have wondered at. In hope it shall not,

Olivia Yes, my lord, this is he. How are you, Malvolio?

Malvolio Madam, you have wronged me. Scandalously wronged me.

Olivia Have I, Malvolio? No.

Malvolio Lady, you have. Please read through that letter. You cannot deny that it is in your handwriting. Write differently if you can, either in handwriting or phrasing; or say this isn't your seal or your composition. You can say none of these things. Well, admit it's yours then and tell me, in simple honesty, why you have given me such clear signs of your favor. You ordered me to come to you smiling and cross-gartered, to put on yellow stockings, to be rude to Sir Toby and the less important people. And when I acted this way in obedience and hope, why have you allowed me to be imprisoned, kept in a dark room, visited by the parson, and made the most scandalous fool and dupe that trickery ever deceived? Tell me why!

Olivia Alas, Malvolio, I did not write this, though I admit it is much like my handwriting. Beyond a doubt, Maria wrote it. And now that I think about it, it was she that first told me you were mad. Then you came smiling, and acting in the ways that had been previously suggested to you in the letter. Please calm yourself. This trick was played on you very maliciously; but when we know why it was done, and who did it, you shall be both the accuser and the judge in your own case.

Fabian Good madam, hear what I have to say, and don't allow a future quarrel or brawl to spoil the pleasure of this present moment, which has astonished me. In the hope that it won't,

365 Most freely I confess, myself and Toby
   Set this device against Malvolio here,
   Upon some stubborn and uncourteous parts
   We had conceived against him. Maria writ
   The letter at Sir Toby's great importance;
370 In recompense whereof he hath married her.
   How with a sportful malice it was followed,
   May rather pluck on laughter than revenge,
   If that the injuries be justly weighed
   That have on both sides passed.

375 **Olivia** Alas, poor fool, how have they baffled thee!

Feste Why, 'some are born great, some achieve greatness, and
   some have greatness thrown upon them'. I was one, sir, in
   this interlude; one Sir Topas, sir; but that's all one. [*Imitating*
   Malvolio] 'By the Lord, fool, I am not mad.' But do you
380 remember? 'Madam, why laugh you at such a barren rascal?
   An you smile not, he's gagged'; and thus the whirligig of time
   brings in his revenges.

Malvolio I'll be revenged on the whole pack of you.

[*Exit*]

Olivia He hath been most notoriously abused.

385 **Duke** Pursue him, and entreat him to a peace.
   He hath not told us of the captain yet;
   When that is known, and golden time convents,
   A solemn combination shall be made
   Of our dear souls. Meantime, sweet sister,
390 We will not part from hence. Cesario, come;
   For so you shall be, while you are a man;
   But when in other habits you are seen,
   Orsino's mistress, and his fancy's queen.

[*Exeunt all except* **Feste**]

I very freely confess that it was Toby and I that set this trap here for Malvolio, because we resented his proud and rude behavior. Maria wrote the letter at Sir Toby's strong urging, in return for which he's married her. The way in which the trick was carried through with a playful malice might arouse laughter rather than a desire for revenge if the grievances of both sides are fairly weighed.

Olivia [*to* **Malvolio**] Alas, poor fool, how they have hoodwinked you!

Feste [*to* **Malvolio**] Why, "some are born great, some achieve greatness, and some have greatness thrust upon them." I took part, sir, in this comedy—I played Sir Topas, sir, but that doesn't matter. [*He imitates* **Malvolio**'s *voice*] "By the Lord, fool, I am not mad." But do you remember? [*He imitates* **Malvolio**'s *voice*] "Madam, why do you laugh at such a barren rascal? If you don't smile, he's speechless." And so the spinning top of time brings revenge around.

Malvolio I'll be revenged on the whole pack of you!

[**Malvolio** *exits*]

Olivia He has been very scandalously mistreated.

Duke [*to* **Fabian**] Go after him, and plead with him to make peace. He has not told us about the captain yet. [**Fabian** *exits*] When that has been dealt with, and the happy time arrives, holy matrimony shall unite us all. [*To* **Olivia**] In the meantime, sweet sister, we will not depart from here. [*To* **Viola**] Come, Cesario—for that's what I'll call you while you remain a man. But when you appear in your woman's clothes, you will be Orsino's wife and queen of his love.

[*All exit except* **Feste**]

237

Feste [*Sings*] *When that I was and a little tiny boy,*
395 *With hey, ho, the wind and the rain;*
A foolish thing was but a toy,
For the rain it raineth every day.

But when I came to man's estate,
With hey, ho, the wind and the rain;
400 *'Gainst knaves and thieves men shut their gate,*
For the rain it raineth every day.

But when I came, alas, to wive,
With hey, ho, the wind and the rain;
By swaggering could I never thrive,
405 *For the rain it raineth every day.*

But when I came unto my beds,
With hey, ho, the wind and the rain;
With toss-pots still had drunken heads,
For the rain it raineth every day.

410 *A great while ago the world begun,*
With hey, ho, the wind and the rain;
But that's all one, our play is done,
And we'll strive to please you every day.

[*Exit*]

Feste [*sings*]

> When I was just a little tiny boy,
>> With hey, ho, the wind and the rain;
> My foolishness was just a toy,
>> For the rain it raineth every day.
>
> But when I came to man's estate,
>> With hey, ho, the wind and the rain;
> To rogues and thieves men shut their gate,
>> For the rain it raineth every day.
>
> But when, alas, I took a wife,
>> With hey, ho, the wind and the rain;
> Blustering didn't help my life,
>> For the rain it raineth every day.
>
> And when my life drew to its close,
>> With hey, ho, the wind and the rain;
> A drinker still had a drunkard's nose,
>> For the rain it raineth every day.
>
> A long time ago the world began,
>> With hey, ho, the wind and the rain;
> That matter's none. Our play is done—
>> And we'll strive to please you every day.

[**Feste** *exits*]

Comprehension   Check What You Know

1. When Act 5 opens, Fabian and Feste are talking about a letter. What is important about this letter?

2. What do you learn about Antonio's past? Why are the Duke and his men angry with Antonio? Why does Viola defend Antonio?

3. What accusations does Antonio make about Viola? Why does this confuse everyone?

4. When Olivia refuses Orsino yet again, what does he threaten to do? Why? What is Viola's response to Orsino? Why?

5. How does the Duke respond when Olivia says that Cesario is her husband? What is Viola's response? How does Olivia prove her claim?

6. Who do Sir Andrew and Sir Toby think they confronted? Who did they actually meet? How does Sebastian explain what happened?

7. How do Viola and Sebastian test each other to make sure that their twin is really alive? How do Duke Orsino and Olivia respond to the news?

8. Why does Olivia decide to have Fabian read the letter rather than Feste?

9. Olivia says that once events are explained, Malvolio must pass judgment on the perpetrators, not her. How does Malvolio react? Why?

10. How does Feste explain the way that he treated Malvolio? What is Malvolio's response?

11. The Duke sends Fabian after Malvolio to make peace with him for everyone's sake. Do you think he'll accept apologies? Why or why not?

Kelly McGillis as Viola with company in The Shakespeare Theatre's 1995 production of *Twelfth Night* at Carter Barron Amphitheater in Rock Creek Park directed by Michael Kahn. Photo by Carol Pratt.

Activities & Role-Playing **Classes or Book Clubs**

Who *Are* You? When Sebastian and Viola reunite, their meeting is handled delicately, carefully, almost as if talking too loudly would make their twin disappear. With three others, read lines 209–281. (Whoever plays the Duke can also read Antonio's few lines.) Experiment with ways to read the lines. Try being excited and loud or quiet and amazed. Have the twins talk only to each other, as if everyone else has disappeared. Then try having the twins make their comments more to the other characters, as if announcing "my twin is alive!" Remember, your goal is to get the most impact from the twins' reunion.

Discussion **Classes or Book Clubs**

1. Critics often talk about "The Malvolio Problem" because they are uneasy about the way Malvolio is treated. Is it funny? Is it funny for a while and then not so funny? Does the treatment of Malvolio spoil the play for you? Explain your answer.

2. All through *Twelfth Night,* the Duke has been very involved with how he feels. Now the Duke has to deal with reality, where his feelings may lead to actions. For a few moments in Act 5 things could go very badly. What do you think of Duke Orsino? Is he a stalker? How does Shakespeare make his audience accept Orsino as a worthy husband for Viola?

Suggestions for Writing **Improve Your Skills**

1. In some texts of *Twelfth Night,* Feste and Fabian are both called clowns, but they are very different. Compare the humor and the attitudes of both men. Consider these issues: Why does Fabian read Malvolio's letter instead of Feste? How do you feel about Feste's final remarks to Malvolio? About Fabian's explanation of events? Which person is more likely to get a positive response from Malvolio?

2. Viola never puts her female clothing back on. Pretend you are Viola, and write a letter to a close friend explaining the advantages and disadvantages of dressing as a man.

3. *Twelfth Night* has an ending like a fairy tale. Everyone marries and there is a distinct impression that they will live happily ever after. However, Feste's final song seems to imply that life is more complicated than that. In fact, many of his songs aren't as funny as we might expect in a comedy. Perhaps the message is that events in life are both serious and funny at the same time—it's just a matter of looking at them in a certain way. Write an essay for a student publication, explaining your ideas about why in *Twelfth Night* there is a mix of the serious and the comical.

Twelfth Night Additional Resources

Books

Title: *The Riverside Shakespeare*
Author: J. J. M. Tobin et al. (editors)
Publisher: Houghton Mifflin
Year: 1997
Summary: This volume features all of Shakespeare's plays along with 40 pages of color and black-and-white plates. Each play is introduced by scholarly commentary from one of the volume's editors. The book also contains general background material on the Shakespearean stage and Elizabethan history.

Title: *The Complete Works of Shakespeare*
Author: David Bevington (editor)
Publisher: Addison-Wesley Publishing Company
Year: 1997
Summary: This book offers the complete, unabridged works of Shakespeare as edited by the current president of the Shakespeare Association of America. Editor David Bevington also provides an introductory essay for each play and a general introduction to Shakespeare's life, times, and stage.

Title: *Shakespeare: A Life*
Author: Park Honan
Publisher: Oxford University Press
Year: 1999
Summary: Using the little available data that exists, Honan pieces together this biographical account of Shakespeare's life.

Title: *A Shakespeare Glossary*
Author: C. T. Onions (editor)
Publisher: Oxford University Press
Year: 1986
Summary: This classic reference book defines all of the now-obscure words used by Shakespeare in his plays and shows how the meaning of words that are still common may have changed. The book provides examples and gives play locations for the words.

Title: *Shakespeare A to Z: The Essential Reference to His Plays, His Poems, His Life and Times, and More*
Author: Charles Boyce
Publisher: Facts on File
Year: 1990
Summary: This book features over 3,000 encyclopedic entries arranged alphabetically. It covers several areas of Shakespeare, including historical background, play synopses, entries for individual characters, and critical commentary.

Title: *The Shakespearean Stage: 1574–1642*
Author: Andrew Gurr
Publisher: Cambridge University Press
Year: 1992 (3rd edition)
Summary: An overview of Shakespearean staging by Andrew Gurr, one of the foremost experts in this area. The book highlights the many different theater companies of the day and how they performed.

Title: *Shakespeare's Book of Insults, Insights & Infinite Jests*
Author: John W. Seder (editor)
Publisher: Templegate
Year: 1984
Summary: This entertaining book covers several categories of jabs and mockeries taken straight from the text of Shakespeare's plays.

Title: *The Meaning of Shakespeare* (2 volumes)
Author: Harold Goddard
Publisher: University of Chicago Press
Year: 1960
Summary: Originally published in 1951, this classic, hefty work of Shakespearean criticism includes essays on all of Shakespeare's plays. (Note: Since Goddard's work is in two volumes, readers who seek information on particular plays should make sure they obtain the volume containing commentary on that play.)

Title: *Twelfth Night: A User's Guide*
Author: Michael Pennington
Publisher: Limelight Editions
Year: 2000
Summary: Particularly useful for performers, Pennington's book gives detailed scene descriptions and explains how the play works on a stage.

Videos

Title: *Twelfth Night*
Director: Trevor Nunn
Year: 1996
Summary: A recent version of the play, with the action updated to the 1890s. Starring Helena Bonham Carter and Richard E. Grant.

Title: *Shakespeare and the Animated Tales—Twelfth Night*
Director: Mariya Muat
Year: 1992
Summary: An animated version of *Twelfth Night.*

Audiotapes

Title: *Twelfth Night: From Shakespeare Stories*
Producer: Chivers Audio Books
Year: 1999
Summary: A dramatic reading of *Twelfth Night.*

Title: *Twelfth Night*
Producer: Penguin Audiobooks
Year: 1998
Summary: This is an abridged version of the play.

Title: *Twelfth Night*
Producer: Harper Books
Year: 1990
Summary: A full-length version of the play.

Web Sites

URL: *www.rdg.ac.uk/globe/research/research_index.htm*
Summary: Associated with The Globe Theatre's web site, this collection of research links offers information on the building and rebuilding of The Globe, Shakespeare's relationship to the theatre, and miscellaneous articles on theatrical traditions and practices during Shakespeare's time.

URL: *www.tech-two.mit.edu/Shakespeare*
Summary: MIT's Shakespeare web site; offers full text of the plays in a searchable format.

URL:
http://www.english.wayne.edu/~aune/2200W00Contents.html
Summary: This site offers introductory information for students studying Shakespeare. Offerings include tips for reading and writing about Shakespeare as well as information on individual works.

URL: *http://daphne.palomar.edu/Shakespeare/*
Summary: "Mr. William Shakespeare and the Internet" offers a wide variety of links to other Shakespeare sites. "Criticism," "Educational," and "Life & Times" are just a few of the categories offered.

Software

Title: *Shakespeare Trivia*
Developer: Cascoly Software
Grades: All
Platform: Windows
Summary: A trivia game for any ability or knowledge level. Test your knowledge of Shakespeare; program includes 37 plays, over 1,200 characters, over 400 scenes, and 500 individual quotes. Allows the player to choose the difficulty and type of question.

Title: *Shakespeare's Language*
Developer: Randal Robinson and Peter Holben Wehr
Grades: 9–12, college
Platform: Mac
Summary: This program helps a reader identify, classify, and respond to causes of difficulty in Shakespeare's language. It helps the reader work effectively with syntactical difficulties, unfamiliar words, figurative language, unexpected and multiple meanings of words, and special connotations of words.

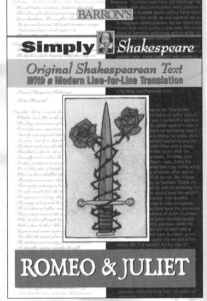

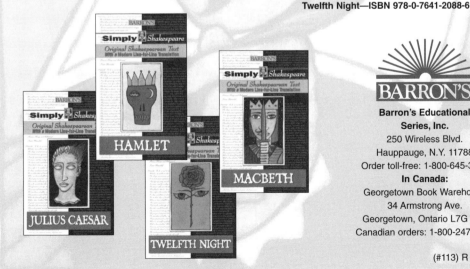

It's Almost Like Seeing the Play!

Shakespeare's immortal dramas are also exciting theater—and adapting these plays into graphic novels is a great way to introduce Shakespeare to younger English literature students. The three titles in Barron's *Picture This! Shakespeare* series combine dramatic graphic novel illustrations with extensive passages from Shakespeare's original texts. Approaching the plays in these books, students take an important first step in appreciating three of the greatest plays ever written. Each graphic novel includes a short summary explaining the play and an illustrated cast of characters.

Each graphic novel: paperback, $8.99, *Can$9.99–$10.99*

ISBN: 978-0-7641-3524-8

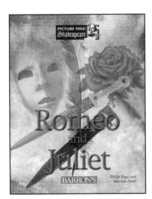

ISBN: 978-0-7641-3144-8

ISBN: 978-0-7641-3147-9

Available at your local book store or visit **www.barronseduc.com**

Barron's Educational Series, Inc.
250 Wireless Blvd.
Hauppauge, N.Y. 11788
Order toll-free: 1-800-645-3476
Order by fax: 1-631-434-3217

In Canada:
Georgetown Book Warehouse
34 Armstrong Ave.
Georgetown, Ontario L7G 4R9
Canadian orders: 1-800-247-7160
Order by fax: 1-800-887-1594

Prices subject to change without notice.

(#157) R7/16

At last! Shakespeare in Language everyone can understand...

SHAKESPEARE MADE EASY Series

Scene 7

Macbeth's castle. Enter a **sewer** *directing divers servants. Then enter* **Macbeth**.

Macbeth If it were done, when 'tis done, then 'twere well
It were done quickly: if th' assassination
Could trammel up the consequence, and catch,
With his surcease, success; that but this blow
5   Might be the be-all and the end-all here,
But here, upon this bank and shoal of time,
We'd jump the life to come. But in these cases
We still have judgement here: that we but teach
Blood instructions, which being taught return
10 To plague th'inventor: this even-handed justice
Commends th'ingredience of our poisoned chalice
To our own lips. He's here in double trust:
First, as I am his kinsman and his subject,
Strong both against the deed: then, as his host,
15 Who should against his murderer shut the door,
Not bear the knife myself. Besides, this Duncan
Hath borne his faculties so meek, hath been
So clear in his great office, that his virtues
Will plead like angels, trumpet-tongued, against
20 The deep damnation of his taking-off;
And pity, like a naked new-born babe,
Striding the blast, or Heaven's cherubin, horsed
Upon the sightless couriers of the air,
Shall blow the horrid deed in every eye,
25 That tears shall drown the wind. I have no spur
To prick the sides of my intent, but only
Vaulting ambition, which o'erleaps itself,
And falls on th'other –

Scene 7

A room in **Macbeth's** *castle. A* **Butler** *and several* **Waiters** *cross, carrying dishes of food. Then* **Macbeth** *enters. He is thinking about the proposed murder of* **King Duncan**.

Macbeth If we could get away with the deed after it's done, then the quicker it were done, the better. If the murder had no consequences, and his death ensured success...If, when I strike the blow, that would be the end of it – here, right here, on this side of eternity – we'd willingly chance the life to come. But usually, we get what's coming to us here on earth. We teach the art of bloodshed, then become the victims of our own lessons. This evenhanded justice makes us swallow our own poison. [*Pause*] Duncan is here on double trust: first, because I'm his kinsman and his subject (both good arguments against the deed); then, because I'm his host, who should protect him from his murderer–not bear the knife. Besides, this Duncan has used his power so gently, he's been so incorruptible his great office, that his virtues will plead like angels, their tongues trumpeting the damnable horror of his murder. And pity, like a naked newborn babe or Heaven's avenging angels riding the winds, will cry the deed to everyone so that tears will blind the eye. I've nothing to spur me on but high-leaping ambition, which can often bring about one's downfall.

Shakespeare is Made Easy for these titles:

As You Like It (978-0-7641-4272-7) $6.99, *Can$8.50*
Hamlet (978-0-8120-3638-1) $6.95, *NCR*
Julius Caesar (978-0-8120-3573-5) $6.99, *NCR*
King Lear (978-0-8120-3637-4) $6.99, *NCR*
Macbeth (978-0-8120-3571-1) $6.99, *NCR*
The Merchant of Venice (978-0-8120-3570-4) $6.99, *NCR*
A Midsummer Night's Dream (978-0-8120-3584-1) $6.99, *NCR*
Much Ado About Nothing (978-0-7641-4178-2) $6.99, *Can$8.50*
Othello (978-0-7641-2058-9) $6.95, *Can$8.50*
Romeo & Juliet (978-0-8120-3572-8) $6.99, *NCR*
The Taming of the Shrew (978-0-7641-4190-4) $6.99, *Can$8.50*
The Tempest (978-0-8120-3603-9) $6.95, *NCR*
Twelfth Night (978-0-8120-3604-6) $6.99, *NCR*

Available at your local
book store or visit
www.barronseduc.com

A simplified modern translation appears side-by-side with the original Elizabethan text...plus there's helpful background material, study questions, and other aids to better grades.

Yes, up-to-date language now makes it easier to score well on tests *and* enjoy the ageless beauty of the master's works.

Barron's Educational Series, Inc.
250 Wireless Blvd.
Hauppauge, N.Y. 11788
Order toll-free: 1-800-645-3476
Order by fax: 1-631-434-3217
Prices subject to change without notice.

In Canada:
Georgetown Book Warehouse
34 Armstrong Ave.
Georgetown, Ontario L7G 4R9
Canadian orders: 1-800-247-7160
Order by fax: 1-800-887-1594

Each book: paperback
NCR = No Canadian Rights

(#16) R 1/14

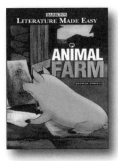